New Games
for the
Whole Family

By the Same Author
California (without grapefruit)

New Games
for the
Whole Family

Dale N. LeFevre

A Perigee Book

Perigee Books
are published by
The Putnam Publishing Group
200 Madison Avenue
New York, NY 10016

Quote from *To Hear the Angels Sing* by Dorothy Maclean, copyright © 1980, reprinted by permission of the Findhorn Foundation.

Quote from *Tao Te Ching* by Lao Tsu reprinted by permission of Alfred A. Knopf, Inc.

Quotes from *Zen Mind, Beginners Mind* by Shunryu Suzuki reprinted by permission of John Weatherhill, Inc.

Quote from *The Animals Came in One by One* by Buster Lloyd-Jones reprinted by permission of Martin Secker & Warburg Limited.

Quote from Robert A. Heinlein reprinted by permission of Robert A. Heinlein.

Quote from Jane Roberts reprinted by permission of Prentice Hall Press.

Quote from *Finite and Infinite Games* by James P. Carse, copyright © 1986 by James P. Carse, reprinted by permission of The Free Press, a Division of Macmillan, Inc.

Quote from "Metalogue: About Games and Being Serious" by Gregory Bateson first appeared in *ETC.: A Review of General Semantics,* Vol. X, No. 3 (1953), reprinted by permission of the International Society for General Semantics.

Quote from *The Mind of Clover* by Robert Aitken, copyright © 1984 by Robert Aitken, published by North Point Press and reprinted by permission.

Library of Congress Cataloging-in-Publication Data

LeFevre, Dale N.
  New Games for the Whole Family / Dale N. LeFevre.
    p. cm.
  1. Games. I. Title.
GV1201.L455   1987   87–26012 CIP
794—dc19
ISBN 0-399-51448-1

Printed in the United States of America
20 19 18

Cover design by Mike McIver

Acknowledgments

I am grateful to the following people for their assistance in the writing of this book:

>Ray Wilkins, Crete, Greece
>Shoshana Tembeck, Oakland, CA
>Barbara Naiditch, San Francisco, CA
>Jill Iggulden, Cape Town, Republic of South Africa
>Anne Lavelle, Amsterdam, Holland
>Todd Strong, San Francisco, CA

Photography (and where pictures are taken):

>David Cairns, Findhorn Foundation, Scotland: pp. 60, 83, 93
>Bill Carter, Bombay, India: pp. 20, 78, 149
>Per Frisk, Stockholm, Sweden: pp. 27, 34, 40, 43 (top), 47, 51, 57 (left), 61, 62, 63 (top, bottom), 77, 85, 87, 95 (top, bottom), 99, 100, 101, 102, 103, 107, 108, 109, 111, 112, 113, 116, 117, 128, 129, 130, 131, 132, 139, 140, 147
>Natalie Goldsmith, Durban, Republic of South Africa: pp. 23, 24, 31, 43 (bottom), 44, 56, 57 (right), 58, 62, 68, 76, 79 (top, bottom), 92, 110, 133
>Dale LeFevre, Adelaide, Australia: pp. 48, 49 (middle, bottom), 65, 67
>Keith Marcum, San Francisco, CA: pp. 45, 106, 162
>Greg Monro, Sydney, Australia: p. 49 (top)
>Virginia Poole, Sitia, Crete, Greece: pp. 86, 89
>Peter Riley, Gawcott, England: p. 115 (top, bottom)
>Claudette Renner, Stockholm, Sweden: pp. 2, 10
>Rüdiger Voss, Geneva, Switzerland: p. 152 (top, bottom)
>Virginia Sajan, San Francisco, CA: pp. 4, 8, 38 (bottom), 41, 50, 52, 80, 84 (top, bottom), 114, 135
>Christian Wopp, Oldenburg, West Germany: pp. 104 (top, bottom), 105

Developmental Skills Section:

>Diederich Sielken, Ursula (Kuhn) Jakobs, Cologne, West Germany

Special thanks for computer time:

>George Sladek, Jr., Rolling Meadows, IL
>Sabine Kurjo, London, England
>Gerald Pfitzer, Cape Town, Republic of South Africa
>Todd Strong, San Francisco, CA
>Mike and Elisabeth Hussy, Gawcott, England

This book is dedicated to my father, Marvin E. LeFevre.

Contents

From the moment I picked your book up until I laid it down I was convulsed with laughter. Someday I intend reading it.

Groucho Marx

Last 19 Minutes

Traveling six days straight-
now down to those
last nineteen minutes
and wondering what
it's all about.

Am I crazy
or merely insane.
NOT insane!
so I must be
C R A Z Y.

Taxi Bus Boat
Taxi Train Boat
Train Train Train
Tram, not insane, man,
    not insane.

                    dale, 8 May 81

This poem was written on a journey from Jerusalem to Bochum, West Germany, where I was presenting a workshop. I started with $30, a boat ticket, a Eurail Pass, and just enough time to make it.

I will ask you to do tremendously simple things.
    We've lost the art of doing simple things, everybody
wants something complicated. Some great target to reach,
some great goal.
    The biggest goal ever reached.
    It's hard sometimes, to do something simple like this.
You have to be children again.
You have to learn to walk again, because this does not lie
    on the ways of your education and your knowledge.
You have to be open to any crazy thing happening and not let
    the mind come in and say what are people going to think
    about what I'm up to now?

This is meaningless.
Let it be meaningless.
It's so simple.
Just drop the thoughts, so complex, so anxious and just be
terribly simple . . .
And if you find it difficult to get started, then just stand
there.
Breathe a little deeper than you normally do.
And when the movement starts to happen just become
tremendously
aware
of the movement, the
extreme edge of the movement,
as if you're standing on the front fender
of a train that's moving along the rails,
whhoosssh
and you haven't got time to watch
in advance, so fast
the view is always changing
and you are right there standing on the front of the train.

Michael Barnett

The teaching which is written on paper is not the true teaching.

Written teaching is a kind of food for the brain. Of course it is necessary to take some food for your brain, but it is more important to be yourself by practicing . . .

Shunryu Suzuki

A Personal Note From the Author

Quite often I'm asked how I got involved with playing and teaching cooperative games. The story is my own continuous miracle.

It starts in the spring of 1974, when a psychic told me that by the end of the year I would be leaving my job and moving to the west coast of America. I had no reason to believe her, since I was very happy with my situation at the time. I lived beside a lake surrounded by beautiful countryside. My job as a Student Affairs administrator was well paid and fulfilling. I had a good rapport with the students and my supervisor had given me an extremely high evaluation. There appeared to be nothing that would cause my departure. In addition, I was becoming security conscious about holding onto my job since at that time work was getting difficult to find. I regarded the psychic's prophesy as a nice vision to hold (for years my secret desire had been to move to San Francisco), but not very likely to happen.

"How'd You Get Into These Games?" "By Getting Fired and Watching T.V."

However, in September, lightning struck. After getting off to a fine start, my supervisor started saying he wanted to fire me!

I was shocked. After a traumatic period lasting a few weeks, I decided to resign. Although I was shattered, I now began actively putting energy into the vision the psychic had given me: I wrote to about ten communes/free schools in the western U.S. asking about living/job opportunities. Some replied though none inspired me, and I prepared unenthusiastically to choose one that might best suit me.

Then, one Sunday in late October, a ray of inspiration shone through my despair. Although critical of American commercial television generally, I was watching an excellent children's program called, appropriately enough, "Make a Wish." Indeed. During that day's show my wish to find something that captured my imagination was answered by a five minute film clip called "New Games." What I saw were people of all ages playing together and having a ball. When it was over, I spoke aloud with wide-eyed enthusiasm, "That's what I want to do!"

Why Not!

The next day I phoned the producer of the show, Peter Weinberg, in New York City and asked him where the New Games people were located. He replied, "San Francisco." Perfect. Of all the places I could have gone, this was my first choice, though it had seemed unlikely I'd really be able to go there.

A short time later I sent a letter, resume and picture to the New Games Foundation, a nonprofit educational organization, asking them about work. Two months passed during which I heard nothing. For a time I forgot about it; then, just as I'd started to wonder if I should write again, a phone call came "Do you want to train with us?" "Sure!" A week and a long cross-country drive later I arrived in San Francisco with just a backpack.

The first night I spent in California, I stayed with friends in Corona Del Mar, near Los Angeles. The next day, the first of February, a warm sun rose. We went to Laguna Beach, which featured tidepools with aquamarine sea anemones, bright purple sea urchins, and other beautiful sea critters. After having crossed a very cold continent in the heart of winter, all I could say was "I'm not leavin'!" Somehow I would find a way to stay in California, even though I had been invited to stay with the New Games Foundation for only two weeks.

"Open Your Golden Gate"

When I first arrived in San Francisco, I went straight to director Pat (now called "Rose") Farrington's home near the Haight-Ashbury district.

I was "greeted" by two mangy, barking, mongrel sheep dogs (ironically, the least intelligent one was named "Stewart," after Stewart Brand, the originator of New Games). Pat's children were there but they didn't pay much attention to me; it seems I wasn't the first visitor to turn up out of the blue. The flat was minimally furnished—what I would call a neo-hippie pad, which had just become my style. In any case, I was far too excited to get discouraged at that point.

Finally Pat arrived along with the Foundation staff, even though it was a Sunday. It was more like a family than a business. We went to the warehouse office where we, would you believe, played a bit! Whatever else might be said about those early days, we did play a lot whenever we needed a breather from work.

My vision of the New Games Foundation was very different from what I found. I had expected the well-organized ongoing concern that it later became. What I found was a loosey-goosey group with a lot of enthusiasm but little organization and even less money. In other words, no money. In fact, they were even borrowing funds to cover basics like rent and phone.

As the first week passed, I thought of how I could extend my stay. Just then, Pat told me that the only real way to learn what New Games were all about was to organize a festival, and they just happened to have one planned for May. Nirvana! I tried not to show my excitement but readily agreed. The arrangement fulfilled both our needs—mine to do something I truly loved and hers to get a volunteer worker with a regular income. (At the time I was drawing unemployment benefits.) Thus began my new career as a games person.

Meet the "Creator"

Since then it has taken me to the brink of my most far-fetched fantasies. Along the way I've met some seemingly mythical people such as Stewart Brand, originator of New Games and editor of the Whole Earth Catalogue series and the *Whole Earth Review* (formerly *CoEvolution Quarterly*). I first got to really know Stewart after two years at the New Games Foundation when he called to ask if he could borrow our Earth Ball, a six-foot inflatable canvas globe. He said he wanted to take it to Oregon for a "Poetic Hoo-Hah" featuring writer William Burroughs. When Stewart told me that the event organizer was Ken Kesey, author of *One Flew Over the Cuckoo's Nest* (whom I'd made a personal vow to meet one day) I replied, "Sure, you can have the ball. Can I come with it?"

Stewart agreed.

Later I learned that Ken was the fellow who had come up with the idea for the Earth Ball, which had since become a key symbol for New

Games. He met us at the train station in a Pontiac convertible complete with a two-person video crew conducting a mobile interview while Ken drove. The fun had begun.

I've met many other mythical and magical people as well while presenting New Games. Perhaps my most unlikely meeting was with Dr. Jonas E. Salk, discoverer of the polio vaccine, in Stockholm during the summer of 1982. Dr. Salk had been a legend to me ever since I was a child for, twenty-two years earlier, I had graduated from Jonas E. Salk Junior High in Rolling Meadows, Illinois. After I had told Dr. Salk that I was traveling and teaching cooperative games, he commented to my friend "We need more people doing things like that." This touched me deeply.

Next Stop

I have also traveled far and wide—so far I've played all over the U.S., in Canada, every major country in Western Europe, Greece, Israel, Egypt, South Africa, Japan, Australia, New Zealand and India. Sometimes my meals have been like this: a Danish pastry in Copenhagen for breakfast and Swedish meatballs in Stockholm for dinner. Although I'm not much of a sightseer, the most amazing things I've seen were the pyramids on the outskirts of Cairo *and* the Taj Mahal under a full moon in Agra, India—during the same week!

I've been able to go to all of these places because games can be fun for everyone. That's my basic message, and most people are receptive. Cooperative games are a universal language. Players of all languages seem to enjoy New Games, even when players don't speak each other's language.

People in the various cultures I've been in respond similarly to the games. While Scots people, for example, were friendly and talkative, they found it difficult to touch each other. Nevertheless, after a half hour of games, this cultural taboo was much less in evidence. I had graded the games by the amount of touching involved so that the process of moving through cultural conditioning could be done in a series of steps, rather than all at once. In the Mediterranean countries and particularly in India, men hugged and women went arm in arm in public, but there is a strong taboo against persons of the opposite sex touching openly. Again, this was largely dispelled after using the same "formula."

Israel presented a fantastic challenge: bringing Jews and Arabs together through play. It was only after I arrived that I realized that getting Jews to play with other Jews was an even bigger challenge. The difference in cultural backgrounds (they came from all over the globe!) made the competitiveness between groups hard to overcome; on the other hand, the culture of the local Arabs is similar to that of Jews from Middle Eastern countries (Mizrahi Jews).

In practice, this meant everybody was talking at once, trying to be heard above the others. This made presenting games in my normal manner impossible—my game introductions were going almost unnoticed at the first games session I did at a Jerusalem community center. I realized that I was going to have to do something dramatic, and fast! Without time to think, I intuitively started flailing my arms and legs in the air and screeching like a maniacal monkey. It worked. ("Crazy" people are given attention all over the world since nobody knows quite what to expect.) As soon as I had everyone's attention, I started to introduce a game.

My main problem in Northern Ireland was not getting Protestants and Catholics to play together but just keeping my composure while on the way to the play sessions. While driving through the various towns, I saw squads of British troops suddenly appear with rifles in hand, apparently ready to fire at a moment's notice. Their steely glances pierced me. In this regard, my co-worker Eamon was no help either. On our route he would casually point out all the gaping holes where buildings had been bombed. In some areas this was every third structure. I arrived at several sessions more in need of New Games than the participants.

Say What?!?!

Incidentally, I found that British English is almost 20 percent different from American English and that this definitely must be taken into account when communicating. I learned not to say, "Do you like my suspenders?" which is their word for garters! And I came to understand that when someone said, "Shall I knock you up in the morning?" they

were not proposing to make me pregnant but to come see me early the next day.

I have found that some real differences between people are closely related to their professions or roles in society. For instance, humanistic psychologists generally love body-contact games. (In fact, it's hard to stop them once they get going!) Business people are often the most enthusiastic players. Teachers usually do the things they tell their students not to do. Housewives are initially fairly reluctant to risk looking silly. People who are considered social outcasts, such as youth gang members and young prisoners, frequently come up with the most creative suggestions for changing games. But equally as often, groups surprise me with their response.

That makes it interesting for me—I must find and tickle a group's "funny bone," so to speak. I have the belief that cooperative games will work with any group of people, and I'm always on the lookout for a group I know nothing about for a new challenge. This can mean going to a new country, such as South Africa, where I was invited to bring players of different races together; or new situations, such as playing with business people in normal business dress, as I did in Stockholm in the autumn of '81. (I couldn't help but laugh when I saw them running crazily back and forth waving their arms in the air yelling "Weee-ooo, weee-ooo," pretending to be fire engines.)

Germany was the first country where I tried to work in a language I did not know. I had one night to learn a little German and actually might have done better sticking to English. Due to mispronunciation, "Make a circle" became "Make a crisis" (though perhaps this came closer to the truth of what really happened). I found that mime, gestures and translating the names of the games gave participants a better sense of what was coming. There was some confusion, but presenting became a game in itself.

Most young Europeans understand a fair amount of English. It is a requirement in their schools because it's often used in business. In any case, those who understand translate for those who don't.

How Playing Is for Me

My focus has gone from rediscovering playfulness to finding that the spirit of play is an invaluable part of my total spirit. It's a way to make contact with my true being. My life is becoming a game of spiritual discovery. The road has been long, but the distance was short: I had only to look within. Pain paved the way for growth as much as joy. I've been learning how to work with energy and realize that there is no good or bad. There is just energy, and how I put it out is how it comes back to me. The way I interpret it determines how it affects my life. And the miracle of discovery continues!

There are at least two kinds of games. One would be called finite, the other infinite. A finite game is played for the purpose of winning, an infinite game for the purpose of continuing the play.

The rules of a finite game may not change; the rules of an infinite game must change

Finite players play within boundaries; infinite players play with boundaries.

The finite player aims to win eternal life; the infinite player aims for eternal birth.

James P. Carse

Introduction

"How often do NFL defensive linemen deliberately try to get the quarterback?"

"You always try to get a key player out of the game," said [Hanford] Dixon. "You want to do it legally," he added, "and we did it legally." [Referring to the knee injury San Diego Charger quarterback Dan Fouts suffered when hit on two successive plays by the Cleveland Browns.]

International Herald Tribune

Some people suppose that because competition and acquisition are used in the exploitation of others, enlightened people should seek the ideal of noncompetition and nonacquisition. Many years ago, Anne Aitken and I taught in a private boarding school that was established on the principle of noncompetition. It didn't work. The young people were not stretched; many became lazy; others found destructive, underground ways of competing.

Competition *can* be healthy. After all, conversation itself is a kind of competition, and at its best saves all beings. When the self is forgotten, the play becomes the thing, and everybody benefits. And as to acquisition, Gandhi, and the Buddha himself, had a few possessions. Competition sharpens our realization and certain possessions are adjuncts of life. At what point do they go wrong? ... Competition, acquisition, and possession go wrong when compassion is missing, when *daña* [charity] is disregarded.

Robert Aitken

New Games for the Whole Family is about just that. This book is designed to help you make play a part of your life. Games are not really necessary for this purpose. Spontaneous play is perhaps more fun than anything else, but it doesn't always happen. Since games have the magical quality of focusing people on playing, I am presenting this book as one way to help you get started.

I have included advice, based on my experience, on how to present and use the games, but my first word of advice is: Don't believe everything you read. What worked for me may not work for you, and what I say won't work just might.

A question that sometimes comes up is, "What is so different about these games?" Once you've played them, you'll get a good idea. However, this is also discussed in the next part, "What's So Special About These Games?"

Sometimes it's not the games so much as what you do with them. The difference is a matter of attitude, as conveyed through presentation, or of adapting to a particular group. Detailed guidelines are given on how to do this. The games are only outlines.

I've included games for a few players or for many, in three flexible levels of activity: quiet, moderate, and active. Some name games are included so that players don't have to call "Hey you!" all the time. Also, games for choosing teams are offered as a way of avoiding the unpleasant aspects of choosing sides. Not one piece of equipment is needed for any but the three "newest" games in this book. For convenience, I've made lists of games to help teach various motor and perceptual skills, games to open and end play sessions, and a few resources.

The spirit of play is always present. It is the child within us all.

We could never take anything up like ordinary children. We had to be perfect, to outdo all the other children in the neighborhood. So we had a coach for tennis, an instructor for riding and another for skating and another for swimming. Normally I would have enjoyed them all—but with father in the foreground urging us on there was no fun in any of it. Games of any kind became a duty and a drudgery.

Buster Lloyd-Jones

The system starts here: I got 90 [at school] and my mother and father hug and kiss me, "Did so good, he got 90! MMM, Kiss, Kiss." But that 90 don't mean anything unless you got a 20. And if I'm not a nut, and if 90 gets me loving and kissing, I hope you get a 20, man. I'm gonna hope you fail.

But later on I really jive myself and say, "May the best man win." May the best man your ass! I'm going to win out and get my kissing and hugging!

Yeah. The competitive system.

Lenny Bruce

To be playful is not to be trivial or frivolous, or to act as though nothing of consequence will happen. On the contrary, when we are playful with each other we relate as free persons, and the relationship is open to surprise; *everything* that happens is of consequence. It is, in fact, seriousness that closes itself to consequence, for seriousness is a dread of the unpredictable outcome of open possibility. To be serious is to press for a specified conclusion. To be playful is to allow for possibility whatever the cost to oneself.

James Carse

What's So Special About These Games?

First and foremost, these games are for everyone. I've played with a wide variety of people and have seen old folks and children hugging to become unfrozen from the "Wizard's" spell, families and singles getting all tangled up in a "Giant Knot," mentally and physically handicapped people becoming "Fire Engines," police and prisoners protecting their mutual leaders from the "Detective"—sometimes all these people were in the same game! It's hard for anyone to resist joining.

Some new games are ones you know but haven't played for years or that have been changed to make them new. Others are games you've never seen before, and still others are invented by you. Some games, like "Cat and Mice," are rough while some, like "Captain Video," are gentle and quiet. All are safe.

While a number of the games include competition, no one cares or remembers who wins or loses. There is no pressure or need to win, hence there is no anxiety about losing. People play with one another rather than against one another. Players are not eliminated; they simply change roles and keep playing. No special treatment is given to the winner: "You're the last one left? Great, you can start the next game."

Playing is just as exciting for someone who has played the games many times as it is for the first-time player. The games don't get boring because they are different each time you play them. I'm never sure what will happen! Even though I've introduced some games more than a hundred times and think I know everything about them, players just being introduced to them can sometimes think of a wonderful variation that never occurred to me.

By encouraging suggestions and responding positively to them, I invite everyone to use their imagination. Though rules are given to start a game, they are not chiseled in stone. Everybody's ideas count. Sometimes the ideas flop. So what? Who cares? At least we tried it. We can always go back to what we started with or try something else. Very often, though, we end up with a better game.

No Toys, Just Us!

Unlike many games or activities, all but three of the games in this book require *no* equipment. Gimmicky equipment is expensive and therefore not economically feasible for most people. There are other problems:

stationary apparatus is generally accessible to small numbers, while equipment that can be moved always involves transport scheduling, and all equipment requires maintenance and replacement.

The main ingredient here is the player. People discover how much fun it can be to simply play games cooperatively with each other. A unique sense of community develops where people feel closely connected. They can let go of their normal roles in a supportive atmosphere that allows them to express themselves more freely.

Anyplace, Anybody

These games can be played almost anywhere. In reply to a question from Simon Vinkenoog, a Dutch author, asking whether I could do a few games in his cramped, crowded work room at home, I blurted out confidently, "I can do them in a clothes closet!"

An important aspect I stress is that each player develop a concern for the safety of fellow players so that everyone plays fully but no one is ever hurt. This provides us with a model of cooperative behavior that is constantly reinforced during the games session. Since it doesn't matter who wins, and since by the very nature of these games, players are constantly changing roles or teams, there is little chance to develop animosity.

There are important psychological and sociological aspects to the playing experience. In games where there is no "loser," a person can develop self-esteem and a more positive self-image. There isn't the constant feedback of "You're not good enough." You *are* good enough. All you have to do is join the game.

It doesn't matter if you can't do the action, such as running; you simply do the best you can. No one is judging. Or you can always suggest a change, such as s-l-o-w m-o-t-i-o-n. It doesn't destroy the game as long as the other players are included in making the decision. An alternative that is fun and a challenge can always be found. No one says, "You can't play. Go away!"

When playfully expressing oneself, one relaxes, often unconsciously, and tension dissolves. People who are normally shy, withdrawn or afraid of meeting new people regularly "forget" how they are supposed to be and play without inhibition.

Finally, basic exercises of any kind can be pretty boring boring boring, but when the exercise can be put in the form of a game, it becomes an ad-ven-TURE. Since the elements of the games are highly adaptable, they can be changed to get the desired result. For instance, any motor or perceptual skill can be developed through the use of games. Many of these skills are already a part of most games, and it merely requires finding a game that has the desired movement or discrimination. If one can't be found, you can invent a "new" game! (See the end of the book for listings of motor and perceptual skills involved in the games.)

Hints for Games Leaders

Games facilitation skills generally remain the same: concern for safety, playfulness, enthusiasm and a brief, clear description with a demonstration are still keys to making a game work. However, a games leader outside of her/his "territory" needs to be aware of local taboos, at least initially. Many of these, like not touching, generally melt away as the feeling of warmth increases between participants.

A facility in the art of mime, or at least dramatic gesturing, is of obvious value when presenting games to people whose first language is not the same as yours. Play leaders can also benefit from knowing a few key phrases in the players' language, e.g. "Make a circle," "Form a line," or "Get a partner."

So, how does it work for me? At first, it's generally the same. I walk into a room of nervous people who are very self-conscious about being there. The thought crosses my mind, "How will I ever get these people to play?" Right. This is my ever-present challenge. The simple answer is to start by doing something I find fun. Maybe I will say something like, "I didn't know this was a funeral!" Or throw a sponge Frisbee to an unsuspecting soul at point-blank range. Or I might put on a funny hat. Next, someone smiles, or if I'm lucky, laughs. The ice begins to melt.

Before beginning to introduce games, I always ask people to form a circle. This signals an informal ritual of beginning to the participants. I ask people to close their eyes and remain quiet for a few moments to allow time to tune in to their own playful spirit, to each other, and to the place we are in.

Next, I'll present a game that isn't too physically or psychologically threatening like "Giant Knot," or for kids, "Fruit Basket." If people appear stiff and tentative I stick to games that do not single out individuals because this embarrasses them too much. However, games that are *too* safe are boring—the risk-taking is also part of the appeal.

As the group loosens up, each game becomes a little bit sillier than the last. Introduced at the right time, a very silly game is totally absorbing, even for a very serious group. For instance, people outside Germany told me that the Germans take everything seriously, but I was able to see their playful side, which is actually substantial. The dumb game of "Choo-Choo"—a "train" of people invites others to join them by making cheerleading chants, complete with gestures, of the onlookers' names—was a very effective ice breaker at the German Sports Academy in Cologne. After that, they were ready for anything! Though the group was hesitant to speak initially, fearing they would make a grammatical mistake in front of me, they later began making jokes, which is hard to do in one's second language.

Share-a-Game

People often share new games with me. In fact, one-third of the games in *New Games* come from this source. For example, the game of "Quack!" comes from Englishman Jim McCritchie, whom I met in Geneva, Switzerland; the "Greeting Game" comes from Jeroen (pronounced Ye-ROON) of Eindhoven, Holland; "Cat and Mice" comes from a French boy I met in Aseda, Sweden; and "A-Rum-Sum-Sum" I learned in Germany, only to find variations all over Scandinavia.

Before You Start Playing

Note: I have indicated a range of how many people can play each game, though usually the middle point is the best number of players. When you have more than fifty participants, or if a maximum is indicated, generally it is better to make two groups of the same game or two different games. The latter might be an active and a quiet game, thus giving people a choice. It becomes hard to have a sense of what's happening with so many people, and some games become boring or dangerous with too many participants. However, there are games that lend themselves to groups of more than fifty, and these are indicated as: 50+.

The rules of these games are provided merely as a starting point for playing. Use your own and your fellow players' ideas to introduce and play the games. Your "game" for introducing each one becomes seeing if you can find a different way to do it every time.

Ice Breakers—Games to Start

Energy

Knots/Giant Knot

A-Rum-Sum-Sum

Fruit Basket

Zoom

Games for Closure

Lap Game

La Ba Doo

Car Wash

Dead Lions

Bear Hunt

"What I was going to say," said the Dodo in an offended tone, "was, that the best thing to get us dry would be by a Caucus-race."

"What *is* a Caucus-race?" said Alice; not that she much wanted to know, but the Dodo had paused as if it thought that *somebody* ought to speak, and no one else seemed inclined to say anything.

"Why," said the Dodo, "the best way to explain it is to do it." (And, as you might like to try it yourself some winter day, I will tell you how the Dodo managed it.)

First it marked out a race course, in a sort of circle ("The exact shape doesn't matter," it said), and then all the party were placed along the course, here and there. There was no "one, two, three, and away," but they began running when they liked, and left off when they liked, so that it was not easy to know when the race was over. However, when they had been running half an hour or so, and were quite dry again, the Dodo suddenly called out "The race is over," and they all crowded round it, panting, and asking "But who has won?"

This question the Dodo could not answer without a great deal of thought and it sat for a long time with one finger pressed upon its forehead (the position in which you usually see Shakespeare, in the pictures of him), while the rest waited in silence. At last the Dodo said, *"Everybody* has won, and all must have prizes."

Lewis Carroll

Omni: Why is humor so important?

De Bono: Humor is by far the most significant phenomenon in the human brain because it demonstrates lateral thinking—the escape from the mundane perceptual path to another path. For example, an airline pilot goes for a medical checkup and learns he is in fact almost blind. Still, he wants to fly for another year to get his pension. When the doctor asks him how he's able to land the plane, the pilot explains that he uses the Jesus Christ method: "I point the nose down, and when the copilot screams 'Jesus Christ!' I level off."

Omni **Magazine interview with Edward De Bono**

Games/Gentle Games

Games for Your Bomb Shelter

At Kiryat Schmone, a border town in the Galilee area of Israel, my co-worker Jan Spector, our organizer Iris Mishaeli, and I were actually asked if we knew some games that could be played in bomb shelters, to help ease people's fears and help relieve the tension of waiting for the all-clear signal. A few months later on German television news, I happened to see a filmed news report of Kiryat Schmone under heavy Arab attack. The reality of our preparations struck home.

Energy (5–25 players)

Any time we play games, we need some energy, and this game will give us all we need to start. To begin, we take each other's hands, forming a circle. The energy begins moving around the circle by means of a hand squeeze passing from person to person.

Pass it around one way, then the other. Then, a first test—see if the group can manage to maintain two energy pulses going in opposite directions. That means one person will receive energy from both directions at once and will have to squeeze back with both hands to keep the two energy pulses going.

After managing this, propose a real test of the energy—passing it with eyes closed! After about ten seconds, send two more energy pulses. If you're really devious, you may want to continue to add new energy pulses in less and less time—until you hear laughter (usually in a minute or less)—letting you know that there's enough energy to begin the next game.

Zoom (5–30 players)

If you're sick of getting stuck in traffic jams, wishing you could just zoom past the motionless cars, here's a way you can—in your fantasies, at least.

After the group is in a fairly close circle, pass the word "zoom" around from person to person. It will likely go slow, so as it comes back to you again, you can liken the speed to first gear in a car. Ask the group to try again, a little faster, in second gear. Then third, and fourth. For sports car enthusiasts (and with a small number of players) you might even try fifth gear.

Finally, to make the "car" safe with all this speed generated, it must have brakes. To apply brakes, a player must stick his leg out and step down on an imaginary brake while uttering a braking sound, "E-e-e-ek!" (It's a good idea to have everyone practice this together—it's embarrassing if you have to be the first one to do it alone.

After braking, the car not only stops but goes into reverse around the circle. It may be good to limit players to only one use of brakes so that all drivers get a chance to "Zoom" about. Otherwise, our car may get stuck on one stretch of road, and all the gear changes could wear out the transmission!

Zip, Zap, Pop! (5–15 players)

Snap, Crackle and Pop! were characters in an American advertisement for breakfast cereal. "Zip, Zap, Pop!" won't fill your stomach but will wake you up, since you must be alert to play it.

We sit in a circle facing the middle. One person starts by placing one hand or the other flat on the top of her head with fingers extended saying, "Zip." Whoever is sitting in the direction of where the starter's fingers are pointing goes next. This person can either repeat the action of the starter by pointing in the same direction repeating the word "Zip," or he can reverse directions by placing his other hand flat under his chin pointing back in the direction he received the zip from while saying, "Zap."

Like with so many things these days, there is a third possibility. The second person can also point at anyone in the circle and by saying "Pop," the person pointed at is next. From there on it's Zip, Zap, or Pop!

If anyone should (heaven forbid) make a mistake, for instance, zapping while making a hand motion for a zip, we do not eliminate him. We merely let him know he did it wrong with an "oo" or "ah" or whatever seems appropriate. Then the person who made the mistake starts the game up again.

This game is most fun when you keep a regular tempo going, *at least* one direction a second. Of course, at the beginning it's good to go slow until everyone gets the idea of how the game works. Later, just when everyone seems to have mastered this, suggest speeding up the tempo to twice as fast. While you may sometimes feel zapped, you will rarely be too pooped to pop.

Captain Video (3–20 players)

Since this game relies on a visual message, it probably ought to be called "Television." Boring! *Captain Video* was the first television science fiction show that I saw about space adventure (way before *Star Trek*) and the results of this game are pretty far out in space, so . . . the Captain and his Space Rangers fly again!

In Captain Video, we pass a motion (sometimes with e-motion). The easiest way to do this is to arrange players in a circle and, after demonstrating the game, have them face away from the center. Have one person in the center play Captain Video. The Captain starts by tapping a Space Ranger (second player) on the shoulder, which is the signal for the Ranger to run around.

Captain Video then performs a simple movement, for instance, doing one deep knee bend while winking. The Space Ranger must pay close attention to detail because she must later duplicate this exact motion to the next Space Ranger. The Captain takes the first Space Ranger's place in the circle, but now faces in so he can watch the unusual changes his winking/knee bend goes through.

Each succeeding Space Ranger repeats this process until it reaches the last Ranger. Then the last Ranger and Captain Video step into mid-circle facing each other and, at the count of three, do the motion at the same time. The two are not usually recognizable as the same thing—in fact, they are usually ridiculously different. Who knows? The sight might even make Darth Vader laugh.

Face Pass (2–25 players)

Are you tired of seeing the same old face staring back at you in the mirror? Here is a chance to change it! Arrange the players in a circle so that everyone can see each other. The presenter starts by making a strange or distorted face. When everyone has had a chance to see it, the presenter turns either to her left or right. The second person, after he gets over the shock, amazement or laughter, carefully copies the expression—much like a mirror—and then both face the center so all can see how successful his attempt is.

Finally, the second person slowly changes his expression until he finds one he likes. He then repeats the process by passing his creation to the person next to him (in the same direction). Continue in the same manner in the same direction until everyone has had a turn. After seeing your distorted mirror image, you might not mind your old kisser.

Many Tired Players

Dead Lions (2–50 players)

It's been a rough day. Everybody's hyperactive, making you wish you could send them into hyper-space. You need a rest, fast! But you can't get away just now. You can scream, or play "Dead Lions." (Or do one, then the other.)

In "Dead Lions" the idea is to play dead by remaining as motionless as possible. (Did I hear a sigh of relief?) Have all the players (or lions) except one—the "hunter" from the zoo—arrange themselves so that they are comfortable lying, sitting or whatever. Explain to them that they must play dead so that the hunter won't catch them. If they move and the hunter sees them, they are caught and must join the hunter and help him. Breathing and blinking the eyes are allowed but no other movements. All eyes must be open and visible.

The hunters can do anything to get lions to move *except* touch them (no spitting, either!). You soon realize how hard it is to be silly when you try to be and how easy it is to be silly when you're not trying. In any case, this game should provide a few minutes of relief to your poor addled brain. Maybe more, if everyone wants to play again.

A-Rum-Sum-Sum (2–50 players)

To get most games started, it's necessary to explain some sort of rules. Not so with this one. All you need to do is say "Watch me and join in when you've got it." This game can be done either sitting or standing.

First, there is a little ditty to sing. The words go like this:

A-rum-sum-sum,
A-rum-sum-sum,
Goodie-goodie-goodie-goodie-goodie,
Rum-sum-sum. (repeat)

A-ra-men, a-ra-men,
Goodie-goodie-goodie-goodie-goodie,
Rum-sum-sum. (repeat)

Keep a steady beat. The melody doesn't matter too much—you can make one up. I'm assuming most of you are like me and can't read music, but I've included it anyway.

A Rum Sum Sum

Now comes the hard part—the hand movements. As you proceed to sing out the tune of "A-rum-sum-sum," you slap your thighs with your hands for each syllable. For example, "A" (right hand slap on the right thigh) "rum" (left hand to left thigh) "sum" (right hand, right thigh) "sum" (left hand, left thigh). Repeat this. Next comes the "Goodie-goodie-goodie-goodie-goodie," while alternating hand slaps on your chest for each "goodie." Hang in there!

Follow this with "Rum-sum-sum" back on the legs. Go through the same thing one more time. Then do "A-ra-men, a-ra-men" while deeply bowing with arms extended for each A-ra-men, followed by another "Goodie-goodie-goodie-goodie-goodie, Rum-sum-sum." Do this part, starting with the "A-ra-men" over again to finish. Whew!

Now that you've read the explanation, you see why it's easier to just do it and have everyone follow. As the group learns the chant, you can speed it up each time you do it until the game looks like practice for some sort of weird religious ceremony in triple time.

Ain't No Flies on Us! (5–50 players)

We're the good guys, right? We're so good, flies won't land on us. But you guys! Well, we don't know about that, and we'd like to tell you about it. We can do this by making two lines of equal numbers facing each other about 20 to 25 feet apart.

We, the good guys, start by taking a step toward your line and calmly, politely reminding you of the "facts":

There ain't no flies on us,
there ain't no flies on us,
there may be flies on you *guys, but*
there ain't no flies on us!

"You guys" then take a step toward us and politely and calmly, but just slightly louder, return the same message.

We continue moving closer, step by step, exchanging this chant until we're nose to nose, no longer calm or polite. After "you guys" have a last turn, we might finish by suggesting giving a hug or at least a handshake to the person across from you to show no hard feelings. You'll feel much better for it—remember, it's only a game!

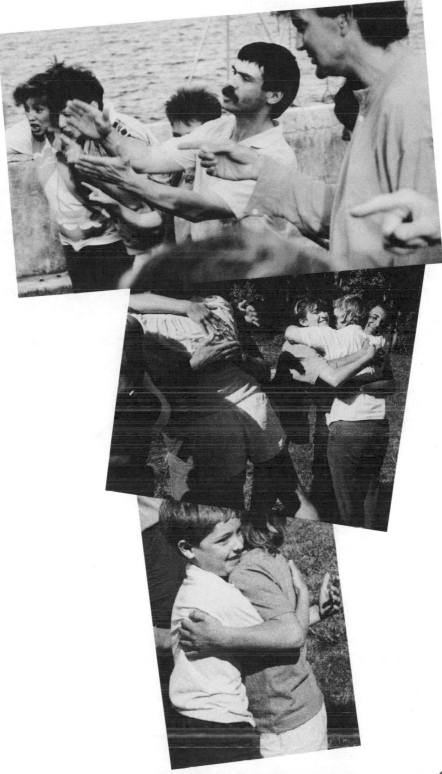

Ironing Board (10–50+ players)

It's time for you and a friend to go out on the town, but wait! Your clothes have some wrinkles and neither of you has time to change. Not to worry, since by some miraculous coincidence you both happen to be wearing the very latest miracle fabric, which only needs smoothing out with the hands of your companion. So while you stand still, your friend slowly runs her hands over your clothes, stroking out all the wrinkles. There, all better!

Now it's your friend's turn. Not only will your clothes be smoother, but you'll also feel much closer to each other.

Quack! (2–50 players)

Some days everything seems upside down. Everyone you meet looks and acts a little strange. "Quack!" is a game that creates these conditions, too, but in a humorous way. In fact, it's one of the silliest games I know.

Everyone stands with their legs slightly apart. Then they let their bodies hang down from the waist so that they are doubled over with their hands holding on to their ankles or knees. While looking between their legs, the players proceed to walk backward. Every time two people touch, they get bum to bum, make eye contact through their legs and loudly proclaim "Quack!" to each other.

Then they move on to a similar encounter with someone else. This goes on for a few minutes until people regain their sanity (or lose their sense of balance) and stand upright again.

"Quack!" is a game I would hesitate to open a session with since it might prove too threatening to people who are not yet in a playful mood. Perhaps you can see why. Once the group is ready, though, this game can really loosen everyone up. Be prepared for anything after "Quack!"

Fitness is no fad. What was once a nation of farmers, then of workers, is now a nation of clerks. Clerks need exercise . . .

John Naisbitt

Sensible people get paid for playing—that is the art of life.

Alan Watts

Life must be lived as play, playing certain games, singing and dancing.

Plato

Can You Make a Living Teaching New Games?

I'm asked this question by well-meaning people at least once a week, often once a *day*, and *sometimes* once an hour. Not only do I *make* a living from New Games, it *is* a living. Although I find myself in a world that doesn't value playing just for fun, individual people sense something worthwhile in what I'm doing, and they respond by coming to play workshops, buying books and videos, all of which support me.

However, if my work was only about games, I would have left it after the first few years. What I've found is that not only is the New Games concept an attitude in relation to play, it can also apply to work. This is not news to those who enjoy their work, but it appears to me that they are in the minority. From what most people tell me, I can only conclude they see their work choices as limited by set patterns they dare not depart from, much like a train on a track. They always have good reasons for maintaining the status quo: a family, job security or preserving a standard of living.

My question to these people is simple, "Are you happy in your work?" It's painful to hear them defend the lives they lead in terms of their responsibilities and fears. But I have to wonder how anyone can possibly give his best to another person or his work if he isn't taking care of himself and his dreams. There has to be a balance. Too often, reluctance to take a risk means becoming stagnant. I believe a little part of us dies then.

Changing my own attitudes about this wasn't easy. As I've already pointed out, I had to get fired to find New Games. In fact, I've been fired three times in all. Each time I already knew I didn't want to stay in the job, but I hung on for one reason or another. A rule of thumb I stuck to was finding something I liked better. These days I listen to my inner voice more and move to projects I want to do before I'm pushed.

I see my work now as an unlimited possibility for living out my most outrageous fantasies. My options are like those of a ship in space— I can go in any direction I choose! What I am suggesting in part is being flexible to ever-changing circumstances, an openness to new ideas, and a willingness to take risks trying out these ideas. By attempting projects I've never tried before professionally—like writing this book, co-producing *The New Games Video,* or arranging a cultural exchange with China—my life is my personal example that little is impossible.

A Little Reality

This does *not* mean that every fanciful thought I have immediately becomes a reality. In my experience hard work is usually needed to give physical expression to my dreams. To illustrate this point, I'd like to describe how the European edition of this book was created. Writing does not come easily to me. Envisaging what I wanted to do wasn't difficult, but it was seven years before I finally got my ideas into print.

When I eventually began writing I wrote intensively for several weeks, then took my efforts to Anne, my first editor. In essence, she said it stunk. Although she was right, my pride was wounded and I gave up writing. It was six months before I had recovered sufficiently. And when Per, who eventually helped me produce the first edition, subsequently asked me, "Why don't *you* write a New Games book?" I was able to say, "Yeah, why not?"

The conditions I set for myself were that I had to have enough time and money plus an island retreat where I could do my writing. Six months later I had all three on the island of Crete, Greece. It was idyllic—I had a place a mile and a half from the nearest town, and it was 100 yards from the sea. After a week of eating Greek salads, drinking the local firewater called raki, and generally partying, I realized I had no more excuses. That scared me. What if I couldn't write well, like before? Finally, I thought, what the heck, I don't want to look back someday and say "I *could* have done it." So I gave it a try. The worst that could happen was that I'd find out I wasn't a writer, and that wasn't news to me, anyway.

A year later, after many revisions, the manuscript was ready. However, despite my best efforts I could not find a publisher. From somewhere very deep inside me I got the feeling that I should take the money that was supposed to get me through the winter and use it to publish the book myself. Logically, this didn't make any sense whatsoever. Finding work, and thus income, is normally very hard for a New Games workshop leader in the winter months. I didn't even have a book distributor. But if I didn't find one I wouldn't be out in the cold; I could stack the unsold books in the shape of a room and live in it.

Finally, three months after the book was printed, Element Books in Britain ordered 500 copies. A few months later distributors in New Zealand and Australia did the same. That book has now been translated into five languages. When I began, I didn't know for certain I could sell more than five copies. There were never any guarantees along the way. Even if it hadn't done well, I had fun watching it grow and take shape. It was my first "child."

Me Now

In essence, I live my life as a New Game, a theme I explore in more depth in a chapter of this book called "Life Is a New Game." This is what I've realized as I've explored different directions that I could take with the games, both geographically and professionally, and also personally and spiritually. When I am truly in touch with myself, everything seems to work out—even things that appear awful at the time.

What I have to remember, no matter what happens, is to keep telling myself "This story has a happy ending." My job is to find it.

I've found out why people laugh. They laugh because it hurts . . . because it's the only thing that'll make it stop hurting.

Robert Heinlein

Games for Your Living Room

Car-Car (2–50 players)

To continue along the theme of cars we started in "Zoom," here's a more active game where players actually can do some driving, even those who don't hold a license.

"Car-Car" starts by having people find a partner of about the same height, one in front of the other facing in the same direction. The front player is the car. He places his bent arms chest high in front of him with palms out and open to act as bumpers, which he may need, since his eyes will be closed. The driver will guide her car by the steering wheel (shoulders) nimbly through traffic with no collisions (we hope). After all, insurance rates are high enough, and if you have an accident, they skyrocket!

After drivers take their cars for a little spin, have everyone freeze and reverse roles. If you don't have an even number of players, ask a threesome to invent a vehicle. Sometimes two vehicles can come together to form trucks. What else can be made?

Car Wash (5–25 players)

(Suggestion: make multiple car washes, one for every twenty-five players.)

Naturally, since we've been "Zoom"-ing our cars around in "Car-Car," they have gotten a little dirty. What they need is, of course (!), a "Car Wash."

Have players make two equal lines facing each other, about one arm's length across. Then, assuming you're on a safe, dry surface, everyone kneels. One person, presumably you if you're introducing the game, goes to one end of the lines and announces what kind of car she is, "I'm a dirty old VW bug," for instance. Then she proceeds down between the two lines on her hands and knees, imitating the car she's chosen.

What kind of car you are and the condition it's in will determine the amount of cleaning done. The above VW bug would receive a thorough scrubbing while a "new" Bentley would be treated most gently.

Meanwhile, the players in the lines do all the things a real car wash would do (but with fingers and hands, not sprayers and brushes), such as spraying soap and water, scrubbing dirt away, wiping the water off, and blow drying to finish (not literally finish, of course) the car. At the end we have a clean, well-scrubbed car. Remind washers to adapt to the different makes of cars and not get too rough of they'll scratch the paint and the owner will demand a refund!

The concept of this game was a little difficult to convey in Israel, where there are no car washes! So we invented the first car massage machine!

Pyramids (6–21 players)

Windmills are a common sight on the horizon in Denmark and in some parts of California. Now we can add pyramids as well, no matter where we live. One way to do this with no expense and with the fastest possible construction time is by using people. Forget automation and plastics. This game is labor intensive. You will need enough people so that you can form rows with at least one more person in each row than the row before, for example, 1, 2, 3, 4, and 5. The rows of people stand behind each other. The bottom row is the largest and heaviest while the top row is comprised of one light person. Have a row of "heavies" lie down on their stomachs, side by side, close together, heads in the same direction. Each succeeding row lies on top of the last until one person lies on top of all. From experience, I've found that twenty-one is about the maximum number that can be in one pyramid without squashing the foundations. Also watch out for the person who sneezes!

The Greeting Game
(4–30 players)

"Hello, how do you do? Good to meet you" is a familiar greeting when we meet new people. It's a pretty mindless, if accepted, ritual. Here's a chance to change all that. In the "Greeting Game" we do what's *un*familiar. No words need be said. We start on our hands and knees. As we meet someone, we can greet them in whatever way we feel at that moment.

It's best not to think about it. Just do it. It could be a purr accompanied with a feline rub, a computer tunneling under a bridge, a gymnastic team from Ringling Brothers Barnum and Bailey Circus, or it could be as simple as a silent nod on a cold dark night. Whatever happens, happens (within legal and moral bounds!).

A group definitely needs to be loose for this game or it'll scare them away. If they're ready for it though, the "Greeting Game" can help bring a group to a highly playful level. Who could be reserved after greetings like this?

Games for Your Front Yard

Little Ernie (3–50 players)

This is a story about Little Ernie and his baby brother, big sister, mother, father, grandmother, grandfather, dog (Bonzo), cat (Preston), and anybody else you want to throw in. (That is, if you have enough players to assume all the roles.)

However many roles you choose, divide the group into lines with that number of people in each line. For instance, if you have five people in the family, make lines with five people—or, members—in them. Assign roles according to a person's place in line—that is, the first person in each line is Little Ernie, the second is baby sister (or who/whatever you choose), and so on. Generally the lines are parallel with space enough for two to pass between them.

The story of Little Ernie doesn't exist yet, which is why you need a storyteller who can make up a story. Each time the storyteller men-

tions a player's role, that person must run around his or her entire line. If the "whole family" is mentioned in any way, they must all run around themselves. While running, players are encouraged to act out the story.

The tale is usually short—only a few minutes long—but what an action-packed thriller it turns out to be!

Detective (10–50 players)

There's a gang on the loose in your neighborhood! Don't worry, though—they're easy to locate since they form a circle and, if their leader can be found, the gang can be stopped. We have sent a detective in the middle of the action to conduct the search. He closes his eyes while the gang leader is silently chosen from the circle.

The gang boss starts by making a motion—something that everyone can do. Gang members try to hide their boss by copying every motion he makes. The detective opens his eyes and tries to find the leader to put a stop to the gang's activities. The gang leader is encouraged to change the motion often. To add to the suspense, the detective has only three chances to find the leader. Once the leader is discovered (or if our Sherlock Holmes is out of luck), he is offered the detective's job. Such is the way of modern justice.

Bear Hunt (5–50+ players)

Bird watching has its exciting moments, no doubt, but let's face it, there can't be much of an adrenaline rush to it. Therefore, for the strong of heart I'd like to suggest a bear hunt. We don't hurt any bears, we just look for one to watch.

First, after seating our hunting party in a circle, we need to "march out into the woods." We can simulate this marching by alternating hand slaps to our thighs, left, right, left, right. Then, the expedition leader can call out a song which the hunting party then repeats, line for line:

Goin' on a bear hunt,
Gonna find a big one,
Gotta keep movin',
It'll be fun!

On the way through the woods, we encounter some situations: a bridge, tall grass, a mountain, and a swamp. With each new situation comes a new verse, as the tempo picks up:

There's (1, a bridge; 2, tall grass; 3, a mountain; 4, a swamp) up ahead,
can't go under it,
can't go around it,
gotta go (1, 3, over; 2, 4, through) it.

After each situation is described in verse, it is acted out in mime. The bridge is crossed by making hand or foot slaps to the floor; the mountain is crossed by grasping high in the air with the arms; tall grass is swept aside by sweeping arm movements in front; and the swamp is gone through with the arms representing the legs squishing through the muck.

Finally, we see a cave! Slowing our "march" down, we start our final verse:

There's a cave up ahead.
It's all dark inside.
Here's something furry . . .
and BIG!
With SHARP POINTED TEETH!!
OH! IT'S A BEAR!!!

Again we mime each line. For the first line, we slow the tempo, as if we are approaching a cave carefully. For the second, we reach out with our arms blindly searching. For the third, we find a patch of fur, which in the fourth line we discover is part of something large, as wide as our arms can stretch. Next we find some teeth with the tip of our index finger.

Upon discovering it's a bear, we rush away using triple-time march hand slaps, meeting with the situations we encountered coming in, but in reverse order: swamp, mountain, tall grass, and the bridge. Finally we march swiftly and safely home. Maybe next time we might consider bird watching, after all.

Goin' on a bear hunt

go-in' on a bear hunt, gon-na find a big one

got-ta keep mov-in' it' ll be fun!

there's a BRIDGE up a-head | can't go UN der it |
(tall grass)

can't go a ROUND it | got ta go OVER it

there's a SWAMP up a-head | can't go UN der it

can't go a ROUND it | got ta go THROUGH it (squish squelch ... ...)

there's a MOUNTAIN up a-head | can't go UN DER it

can't go a ROUND it | got ta go OV ER it! | (heavy breathing)

(pause) (pause)
there's a CAVE up a-head | it's all DARK inside

(pause) (pause)
there's some thing FURRY and BIG, with sharp POINTED TEETH

— — OH! | it's A BEAR!

triple time
let's get OUTA HERE! | over the mountain (heavy breathing)

through the swamp (squish squelch squish) ......

over the bridge .... SAFE AT LAST!

Blind Run (5–25 players)

Life has so much excitement and fear, and so many mysteries and obstacles, that it seems we're running blind at times. In "Blind Run," you literally experience this. The thrill and anxiety are not overwhelming though. The unknown is fun and the barriers gentle.

Players form two lines, facing each other, about six feet apart. They have their hands in front of them to straighten the course in case our blind runner goes astray on the path of life. At one end of the lines are at least two people who are prepared to bring a blind run to a gentle end by patting the runner on the shoulders and hips with their hands. These two *must* pay attention to the runner.

At the other end of the line is the runner, who naturally *enjoys* the thought of sprinting full speed with his eyes closed (until he tries). Most likely everyone will want a chance to know the unknown this way, maybe even more than once, spinning around down the course or even running it backward!

The Enter-Scandinavia-and-Give-a-Workshop Game

For you see, so many out-of-the-way things had happened lately, that Alice had begun to think that very few things indeed were really impossible.

Lewis Carroll

My first trip to Scandinavia in 1980 was like playing a continental-sized board game. As the date approached to leave Amsterdam, Janet Spector (who was my working partner traveling with me at the time) and I discovered our first "turn" was to land on the "bad-steering-on-your-newly-purchased-VW-van" square. Every time we hit a bump in the road, the van, whose name was Arthur van Green, (reflecting his Dutch origin and color), would wobble. This meant we had to draw a "repair" card with a mechanic called Anthony, the friend who sold Arthur to us. Anthony was a good mechanic but a little slow in carrying out his work. Meanwhile, time was running short.

Finally, everything was fixed so that we could go on to our next move. After traveling through Holland and West Germany, we came to our first "ferry crossing" square on our way to Denmark. Next we landed on a square called "Customs" in Rødby.

Our main concern about Customs up until this point was how to smuggle seven bottles of alcohol we planned to give away as gifts. As we pulled Arthur up to the Customs checkpoint, the customs agent, who came out of his office to check us, was shaking his head as if to say, "No." This bode ill-fortune. He started to check Arthur over thoroughly, finally insisting that one tire didn't have enough tread on it.

Move Back One Space

We reluctantly started to change the tire when the agent really began freaking out: it looked like we had just drawn a "return-to-West-Germany" card. Unbeknownst to Jan and me, whoever had owned the van before Anthony had taped over some rust spots on the panels nearest the ground and painted over them. Our trusty agent discovered this and began to tear away the tape, proclaiming loudly, "Your van is finished, kaput! Return to Germany!" We were stunned. We had absolutely no expectation that this would happen, and we had to give a workshop in Stockholm in two days. We felt pretty bad.

At this point, we drew the "agent-is-human" card. No, he did not let us go into Denmark. However, Jan had lost a contact lens, and I told the agent we needed to look for it before we left. He said, "Oh, I'll help you look." Immediately he found it, while we had been unable to. So even though he was kicking us out of Denmark, we were able to experience his human side.

So, moving one square back, we returned to "ferry crossing" and went back to West Germany. While on the ferry, we needed to complete our "repair" card, which was to finish changing the tread-worn tire. As I started to jack up our van, I heard this sickening crunch. While Arthur's frame was good, the places holding the jack were rusted to the point of uselessness. *Nothing* seemed to be going right. In the end we were able to use a hoist at a gas station, which was in fact much easier anyway.

Detour

The next move of our game was to find an alternative path to Sweden, since Denmark was clearly out. Looking at the map, I saw there was a direct ferry from Travemunde to Sweden. However, after checking the prices, which were exorbitant, I took another long look at the map and discovered a place called Sassnitz. This looked much closer to Sweden, and we figured it would be much cheaper. So we proceeded in the direction of Sassnitz without checking the map very carefully.

Shortly after leaving Travemunde, we came to a West German

border guard. This struck us as peculiar, but we rationalized it by thinking it must be because Travemunde was a port town. It was not until we left the guard station and saw the barbed wire fences and soldiers with machine guns that it occurred to us that we were entering *East* Germany, which was where Sassnitz was. Once again, it was time to land on the square called "Customs."

Welcome, Comrades!

The first things the border guard asked for were our passports and car papers. After a frantic search, we discovered these were missing. We apparently had forgotten them at the West German guard post. Oops! This was *not* the best way to make our first entrance into an Eastern Bloc country. I had sudden flashes of spending the rest of my life in jail, with no one in the West knowing what had happened. Fortunately, at this time we once again drew the "agent-is-human" and the "return-to-West-Germany" cards. We drove back, picked up our papers, and got a transit visa to Sassnitz.

The novelty of the East German path to Sweden started with *three* searches of our van and paying a fee to enter. The road was winding, and not lit, with few road signs to guide us, and about every 50 kilometers there was a checkpoint. None of this had occurred in other countries. "Leadfoot" Jan liked to speed and totally missed a 90 degree turn that wasn't marked or lit, nearly causing us to crash. We had drawn a "good luck" card.

Goodbye, Comrades . . . ?

For the last time, we thought we were moving onto a "ferry-crossing" square, but this one had an East German twist. It actually read, "Lose one turn, wait three hours." Although we arrived fifteen minutes before a ferry was to depart, which normally would have been plenty of time, when we asked the border guard, "Can we get on that ship?" he just looked at us and slowly shook his head as if to say, "No way." We didn't understand this and thought perhaps there wasn't really a boat leaving. But there was. No explanations. The guard only said you had to arrive an hour and a half before the next boat.

So there we were, stuck in beautiful downtown Sassnitz, which wasn't so bad, really. Well, let's put it this way, it had an ice cream shop, which made Sassnitz a garden spot in any country, as far as I was concerned. It also gave us the opportunity to see briefly how East Germans lived, which was quite interesting since we had not encountered this before. You could say we drew a "cultural-enrichment" card.

It was our turn to move again, and we found out exactly why we were not allowed on the last ship and why we had been told to arrive early. Once again, we found ourselves on the "Customs" square. Arthur was put through three more security checks, and these were *very* thorough. They checked our gas tank by putting a wire down it, and our New Games brochures were closely scrutinized with many questions being asked. Since old Arthur was stuffed with bags and boxes of our things, this process took a long time.

If You're Blond, This Must Be Sweden!

Finally, we got to the "ferry crossing" square. During the voyage, Jan and I glued the tape back over Arthur's rusty lower panels. Earlier, when we had tried to enter Denmark and had told the border guard we were on our way to Sweden, he had replied, "Oh, they won't let you into Sweden, either." So we were nervous that we would once again be pushed back onto the "ferry crossing" square.

As we drove Arthur to the "Customs" square in Trelleborg, we received a positive shock. This time we were greeted by beautiful blond ladies with smiles on their faces. Nobody asked a single question about our van. They couldn't have cared less. The lady agent who checked our van merely made a superficial perusal, all the while chatting merrily with us about the United States and San Francisco. She didn't even notice any of our six extra bottles of liquor. So, into Sweden we go! But wait, the game is not quite finished.

The "Lose Instructions" Card

After driving for a while, deliriously happy to have finally made it into Sweden, we decided to call the youth hostel where our host had made a reservation to tell them we wouldn't be able to make it that night. We discovered we had just drawn a new card in the game called "Lose Instructions."

After we had made a call from Travemunde the day before, we had left the sheet of paper with the name and phone number of the youth hostel and the name of the contact person for our games session. Suddenly, we didn't know anything! At this point, I became very depressed. Or, more accurately, pissed off.

Rather than keep playing the game and look for a solution, I chose to get upset and blame Jan for leaving the information sheet behind. Fortunately, Jan kept playing—she drew a "Take-a-Chance" card, deciding the only thing we could do is call all the youth hostels in Stockholm to see if they had a reservation for us. Then we could only hope that our contact person would call the youth hostel to figure out what happened to us.

Remember: This Story Has a Happy Ending

Jan called all of the numbers she had been given by the operator, and *none* of them had a reservation for us. There was one place that did not answer. Not knowing what to do, we drove on, holding onto the thought "This story has a happy ending." It was all we had left. At four in the morning we finally had to stop to sleep.

We had planned to get up at six, but we slept right through the alarm until seven, when luckily we woke up. Back on the road we stopped again to call as we entered the outskirts of Stockholm. Once again we asked the operator for all the numbers of youth hostels to see if perhaps we had missed one. The very one that we couldn't get through to the night before had a different number from what Jan had written. This time when we tried it, we found—at last!—it was the right place.

The people at the hostel were incredibly friendly. They gave Jan a long detailed description of how to get to the "youth-hostel" square, laboriously spelling out the strange sounding (for us) names of the streets that all seemed about eighteen letters long. When we got there, they even let us take showers, though we hadn't spent the night. We were informed that Sten, our contact, *had* called the night before and even that morning. However, since the hostel staff didn't know who we were, not having heard from us, they could give him no message.

We made a call to the host of our whole Swedish tour, Nic Nilsson, hoping to connect with Sten that way. Nic was out, so we left a message, "Jan and Dale called." It began to look like the end of the line. Our session was to begin at nine thirty and it was already eight thirty. Close, as they say, only counts in the game of horseshoes. Our only remaining hope was that Sten would make one last try to reach us.

So, having done all we could, we went downstairs to have breakfast. If the game was over, at least we'd finish on a full stomach. Up until this point, Jan had been the one who had been saying, "Oh, I have a strong feeling everything's going to turn out all right. We don't need to worry." I was the one freaking out. At this point, we reversed roles: Jan began losing hope while I miraculously relaxed and said, "Hey, it's going to be all right. You *said* it's going to be all right, and it will be." This calmed Jan.

Meanwhile, we tried Nic's office again. We were informed that while Nic wasn't there, and Sten hadn't called either, someone named Jan Daly had called about New Games. Figuring that here was someone who was interested in our workshop and maybe had a clue where it was, I called the number. At that same time the phone across from me at the registration desk of the hostel began to ring. When the man on duty answered, I discovered I was speaking to him. "Jan Daly" calling *about* N.G.s was Jan and Dale *from* New Games: We had answered our own message! This provided a moment of lightness and laughter that had been sadly lacking in this "game," even if it brought us no closer to our workshop.

Better Late Than Never

We were just finishing breakfast when the man at the desk rushed downstairs to tell us there was a phone call. I flew up and found, with great relief, it was Sten. As we had hoped, he made that one last try before calling the whole thing off. The time was nine fifteen.

Sten picked us up and we gave one of our best workshops, perhaps because we were overjoyed from completing our "Enter-Scandinavia-and-Give-a-Workshop" game successfully. Or maybe it went well because of the fact that we were outside. It was a sunny May day, and anything done in Sweden under these conditions can't fail. We didn't care. This game, at least, was over. And, once again, it proved that every happy ending does have a story.

Everything is funny as long as it is happening to somebody else.

Will Rogers

Games for Your Rumpus Room

Three's a Crowd (6–30 players)

There's an old saying that goes, "Two's company, three's a crowd." This is certainly true in the game of "Three's a Crowd." First, form a circle of pairs, one person behind another facing the center. Then choose an "It" and a "Runner." This is a tag game. No one can stay with more than one other player (that is, a threesome) for longer than a few seconds at a time. The Runner, chased by the It, can join any twosome by standing in front of the pair, but the player farthest from the new arrival

(in this newly created threesome) must suddenly "remember" an important matter elsewhere and dash off.

The new Runner is now pursued by the player who is It. When the new Runner is tired, he can stop in front of another pair, thereby making someone else the third, or the One Too Many, and, therefore, the new Runner. If at any point the It catches the Runner, the roles are automatically reversed. Allow players to go on the outside of the circle only, at least initially.

You can add to the excitement by making the rule that when anyone yells "switch," the pursuer (or It) and the pursued change roles. This keeps anyone from being stuck as the It for too long. Or you can also allow the It to join a twosome, passing on her role to the third person in back.

Whatever you do, "Three's a Crowd" is a game that can go on for a long time with many short term meetings of twosomes. After all, getting to know many people a little bit is better than not getting to know anyone at all. Isn't it?

Fruit Basket (7–50 players)

Although this game isn't strictly for fruitarians, we have only our fruit basket with us for going to market. (As I've traveled in many lands, this game helped me learn the names of at least this one food category.) Each player except one sits on a chair (or something, like a pillow or jacket, to designate their place), and the chairs are in a circle. The person who is going shopping stands in the middle. We ask around the circle and everyone, shopper included, declares what fruit they like the most. It's okay to have more than one of a certain kind of fruit (e.g., 2, 3, 4 or more apples).

The shopper starts his shopping by calling out the names of some fruits, like apple, pear, grapefruit. There are no limits to how many names he can call. When he says "switch" at the end of his list, all the people who have picked a fruit called must leave their places and go to some other place made free by someone else. The shopper, weary from the day's shopping, seeks a seat on which to rest, too.

One person will not find a place to sit, as you may have gathered. She becomes the new shopper and calls out fruits. After a few rounds, the shopper can call "Fruit Basket," and everyone must change place (no fair going to the seat beside you—too easy, fruitcake!). With this addition, the game looks something like a performance by Mexican jumping beans.

This game had such a profound effect on one lady in Chamarande, France, that she became known by her game name: passion fruit. *I* can't say whether she deserved it.

La Ba Doo (5–50+ players)

You can't dance? No matter—this is a crazy dance where no one will ever notice. We start by making a circle with our arms on our neighbor's shoulders. Now try side stepping to the right, left foot following the right after half a beat. Finally, add the melody, which is the same as "Mary Had a Little Lamb," keeping time with your steps.

The "Hey!" should be accompanied by a stamp of the left foot, then we reverse direction repeating the song. After finishing this, whoever's introducing the game can ask the group, "Have you done the La Ba Doo dance?" They should answer, "Yes!" If their answer isn't very enthusiastic, ask again. Next the presenter continues by asking, "Have you done the La Ba Doo dance with hands on head?" "No," should be the reply, since they haven't done it yet. "Let's try it," says the presenter, putting each of her hands on the heads of the two people beside her.

This pattern can be repeated with a number of possibilities such

as fingers on ears, finger on nose, hands on stomach, hands on knees, and hands on ankles to name a few. You can repeat this dance at least five times before people have had enough. The really fun part is making a ritual of asking the dancers after each dance if they have done each of the previous variations before asking about a new one, like so: "Have you done the La Ba Doo dance?" "Yes!" "Have you done the La Ba Doo dance with fingers on ears?" "Yes!" "Have you done the La Ba Doo dance with hands on head?" "No!"

As you can gather, very little dancing skill is required, merely the desire to have a good time together.

La Ba Doo Dance

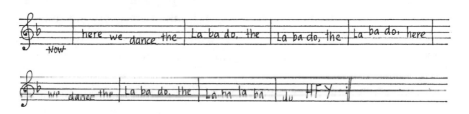

Fire and Trust Leap
(7–25 players)

We hear fire engines 50 floors below us in our highrise building and we wonder where the fire is. So we go to the window and see IT'S IN OUR BUILDING! Quick, grab the kids, walk to the door and open it, walk down the hall for the stairs, go down the stairs, (remembering not to panic or run into other people), go over to a window and open it, get on the windowsill and leap into a safety net.

Actually, we're miming all these motions, which is an elaborate way to lead into the next game of "Fire and Trust Leap." Arrange players in two lines facing each other an arm's length apart. Have the people in each line stand shoulder to shoulder and put their arms out, forming a "net" to catch the trapped fire victim. (Make sure everyone removes watches and other jewelry that could scratch. It would be ironic to "save" someone from an imaginary fire only to have them injured with real cuts!)

Everyone holds out their arms with palms up, alternating arms with the person across from them. (Note: if they hold on to each other's hands it creates very high stress on the wrists when the leaper lands.)

Perhaps it is best to tell people to choose which height they want to jump from, but start low—maybe even at ground level—if anyone is frightened. Later, when we feel more confident, we can leap from higher levels, though I'd stop at around six feet. Now we're almost ready.

Make sure that all the people in the lines have their heads back, out of the way. Insist that jumpers have their arms out in front of them, thereby protecting their faces and spreading their weight over more people. Jumpers should also remove their shoes, especially if hard. Now, when ready, jump! After you have demonstrated the leap yourself (yes, you), have the next person stand at a distance from the end facing the lines.

It is very important to make sure that all the safety precautions are followed and that everyone is paying attention. The first time I presented this game with my co-worker Jan Spector in San Francisco, I didn't notice there were two small boys opposite each other where Jan's head would land. But everyone noticed when she fell through their arms and nearly broke her nose.

Though it can be scary (*I* always hesitate), when you jump and land it feels great. It's nowhere near as bad as it looks. And the leaper is saved from the fire (Where's the fire? Oh, yes, that's where we started this game.)

Games for Your Backyard

Cat and Mice (5–50 players)

One day you find that mice have invaded your house, and though they're cute little fellows, you want to make them go away. For those of you who couldn't kill a mosquito (and that takes *real* love for all God's creatures), there is a peaceful, nay, spiritual solution: transformation.

First, we get a cat. (I know what you're thinking, but wait!) All the mice are on one or the other side of the "room." When the cat says "go," all the mice race to the other side of the room trying to avoid the cat. However, the inevitable happens, and our cat catches a mouse to

whom he does no more than tag. One thing I didn't tell you was that this is a magical cat.

The mouse then undergoes a change not visible in his body, but only through his behavior: He becomes a "mousetrap." He starts catching and holding other mice until the cat can transform them into a "mousetrap," too. By the end, all the mice have been changed into mousetraps! Since some mice have a little more energy and some traps a little more strength than others, remind everyone that while mice can escape if they can get out of the trap, both mouse and trap should try not to damage each other. A change in the way mice and mousetraps move may be required to ensure safety—say to hopping, for instance—and it may be wise to ask everybody to remove jewelry and glasses, which could do harm.

(See, you thought there would be bloodshed, didn't you?)

Fire Engine (10–50+ players)

Do you remember, as a child seeing a fire engine hurtling down the street? Did you ever wish you could be on it? Now you can! In fact, now you can *be* the Fire Engine!

Have the group divide into parallel lines of five or so people, all facing the same direction. Point out a "fire" that is at a point 15 or more yards away. Each of us, as fire engines, must try to put it out. Since it doesn't look like too big a fire, each line at first only sends one engine (person), with siren wailing European-style, "wee-woo, wee-woo, wee-woo!" and lights flashing (that is, one arm flapping above her head).

Upon arrival, the engines take their fire hoses and spray the fire. Each engine discovers that they need help, so they go back ("wee-woo") to get another engine. This is repeated, because it's a big fire getting bigger still, until each line gets all its engines to the scene of the blaze. In Stockholm, men and women in normal business dress played this game, which was quite a sight to behold. Any real fireman would certainly have laughed himself silly watching the spectacle.

Robots (12–50 players)

You now can have your very own robot—in fact, you can have two! Have everybody get into threes—a couple of fours are fine, if the number of people makes it necessary. One person must act as the human robot master who starts up and guides her robots. The robots may only go in a straight line until their direction is changed by the robot master.

If a robot should run into an obstacle, the designated boundary, or another robot, it needs to send out an SOS signal such as "Beep-beep-beep . . ." until the robot master redirects the troubled android. Before starting, the robots and masters can agree on their own unique warning signal to help distinguish them from other robots.

After a minute, have robots and master get together again and pick a new master, and then again, after another few minutes, to give the remaining person a chance to be a robot master. Immediately after this game, I doubt if you'll find many people amongst yourselves who will support automation.

Wizards (5–50 players)

Since play is magical (after all, you were just introduced to a magical cat a few games back), it's time you were introduced to the Wizards. Our magic makers seek to freeze people, but only because they know that other people can unfreeze the frozen with a warm hug.

Have all the players form a circle and close their eyes. Go around and run your hand gently down the middle of the back of those who will become Wizards, with about one Wizard for every five players. Have everyone open their eyes and run to escape the Wizards. The Wizards make the same stroking motion down a person's back to freeze him.

No one knows who the Wizards are at first, even other Wizards, but we soon find out once they start freezing everyone. Of course, everyone is busy hugging frozen players to unfreeze them, making the work of the Wizards harder.

In all fairness and because Wizards like a hug now and again, too, after a few minutes have non-Wizards close their eyes again. You don't even need a circle! Can you believe it! All the Wizards pick other players to become new Wizards, with the same back-stroking motion. Perhaps you wouldn't classify this game as magic, but a hug *has* been known to work wonders!

How to Lead Games

They say the seeds of what we will do are in all of us, but it always seemed to me that in those who make jokes in life the seeds are covered with better soil and with a higher grade of manure.

Ernest Hemingway

(Does that mean that such folks Pile "it" Higher and Deeper—or PhD? Or are they merely full of it?)

He who can, does. He who cannot, teaches.

George Bernard Shaw

Although people in my workshops have thought of 100 or more qualities for leading games, I present here merely a handful of what I feel are the most important ones. Some overlap each other. Most are common sense or at least appear to be, but all too often it's the light pole directly in front of our noses that we walk into, bumping our heads.

Safety Consciousness

The main thing that changes a nonparticipant into a safety-conscious player is the realization that the game is safe. A games leader, in order to create this safe atmosphere, is responsible for looking after both the physical and psychological safety of participants.

This can take **many forms.** For instance, before starting, whether indoors or out, the playing area needs to be looked over for potential dangers such as poles, low beams, table or other sharp edges, holes, glass, sprinkler heads, and animal traces which can be covered, moved or avoided where possible. Once people start playing, they seem to forget that they can hurt themselves. For this reason, **players should be given a warning about these pitfalls before the session begins** with an occasional reminder when appropriate.

The way a game is presented will help determine whether it becomes a game of rugby (or worse) or a game everyone can enjoy safely. The dangers of very physical games can be demonstrated by dramatically exaggerating caution or using mock violence humorously, thereby raising the players' awareness of what they are doing. The general rule is, and this can be stated directly to players: **Don't play so hard that you hurt someone. Use the minimum force necessary.**

When a game starts to get too rough, we can either remind everyone we're there to have fun and not kill each other, or ask, "How can we change this game so that nobody gets hurt?" This refocuses the group on safety. It gives everyone a share of the responsibility for keeping the game safe and also calls on their collective imagination to come up with a solution. Pointing out a few individuals who are playing too rough tends to alienate, and it gives them no chance to recognize and creatively alter their behavior. Handicaps can be created for overenthusiastic players.

While we always want to keep the game safe, there may be times when some players want to play more aggressively. Adults may want to play without children or vice versa. As always with active games, it should be announced at the beginning what kind of game it's going to be, thereby making people fully aware that they can choose not to play. If this is not done, players are sometimes caught up in the spirit of the moment without realizing the danger.

Once you warn people, it becomes their conscious choice to play or not. For instance, at a play session in Govan, a tough section of Glasgow, Scotland, I gave the standard warning that we were about to do an active game and everyone should consider that before playing. The whole time I was speaking I was looking directly at a four-foot, sixty-year-old lady. When I finished she immediately piped up, "Well, you better tell these other people, then!"

Although the discussion so far has been about physical safety, the same ideas also apply to **psychological safety.** If the players sense your concern with their well being, they will trust you and participate more readily. It helps, of course, with a shy or nonathletic crowd, to start with gentle, non-threatening games.

Additionally, I feel **it's very important for a games leader to play the game herself**—the players are more likely to trust and respect your judgment. As a player your attention will be on the game, and you can literally feel if it's getting out of control. As a games leader you notice what is happening to others. A general rule is: **The larger the group, the more attention required from you.** Never hesitate to stop a game when you sense danger. A few times I've waited just a little too long and someone got hurt.

Psychological safety includes letting people know that while they are welcome to join, it's also all right if they choose not to. Besides, someone who is forced into playing usually becomes an energy drain. A teacher working alone with his/her class can offer students who don't want to participate a nondistracting alternative, such as sitting and watching or reading.

I consider disruptive behavior that destroys games as a decision not to play. From experience, I've found that an effective way of dealing with this is to ask the offending player(s) to sit out for at least one game. It should be made clear that she/he is then welcome to rejoin but free to choose. This is a positive approach—the player is not punished so much as excluded for a time from a pleasurable activity he or she has not supported. Self-control is taught through this. (This approach is not usually used with adults.)

To create an atmosphere of psychological safety, a play leader needs to establish order within chaos, setting limits without anger. This means that a clear distinction must be made between the person and his/her behavior. A firm but gentle response is called for and the ability to determine the difference between destructive and creative disruption.

When players are asked to close their eyes for a game, request an observer to take care that no one walks into danger, and let the participants know that they are being watched over. That way they feel more freedom to play.

If someone does appear hurt, any good feelings can quickly disappear. What you as a leader can do is to ask if there is someone who knows first aid (or who can take care of the injured player) while you move everyone else away so that no one stands around staring at the injured player. He/she might only have had the breath knocked out of him/her, and be somewhat embarrassed by the attention.

If the person isn't badly hurt, which is almost always the case, this gives them a chance to recover gracefully. For the rare injury that requires further attention, have at least one person stay with the injured

while another person does whatever is required—gets ice, or telephones for a doctor or ambulance.

Your responsibility as games leader/presenter is to know beforehand where everything that might be needed is, or have available somebody who has the required information. A few minutes of inquiry before the play session begins can save anxiety later for you, the injured party, and the group. If you are co-presenting games, work out between you what to do if someone is injured. Then if an injury happens, you can function smoothly as a team where each leader knows what to do. Meanwhile, the play session can continue with the other players giving a little more thought to safety!

Playfulness

A games leader embodies the spirit of the games he/she presents and plays. If you're having a good time, it'll be easier to convince others to let go and have fun, too. Choose games that you like—this makes it easier to be enthusiastic yourself. Be able to laugh at your mistakes—everyone else will.

Amateur comedians (i.e., almost everyone) can have a field day using stories and jokes in explaining a game. Of course, a lively group will want to join the act, which is always more interesting and challenging and should be encouraged. For instance, once I started a game of "Elephant, Rabbit, Palm Tree" on a day when I happened to be wearing a green T-shirt, bright red sultan pants with little colored hearts on them, an orange baseball hat with a green propeller on top, red- and yellow-striped socks, and brilliant red shoes. Jan Spector pointed at me and said, "This is a palm tree." I dutifully hoisted my arms overhead to demonstrate a "palm." At this point, one of the players responded, "Looks more like a Christmas tree!"

Empowering

When presenting a game, you may find that sometimes players want to change your game or present a game themselves. When this happens,

it's a good idea to keep in mind that it's "our"—not "my"—play session. I advise staying flexible and open to suggestions, except, of course, to things that are obviously unsafe. Even if the idea sounds dumb, it could be a lot of fun. If it isn't fun, that will become apparent. Then you can ask, "How can we change this game to make it more fun?" thereby inviting players to play with the game itself.

Getting Attention

To start a game, it is essential to get and hold the attention of the players. The better focus you have, the more likely that the game will proceed smoothly and be more fun. There will be fewer questions and more involvement. You don't need to become a dictator to do this. For instance, rather than shouting, "Attention, everyone, attention!" you can ask everyone to form a circle, starting it yourself by taking two people by the hands and enlisting their aid. That can be a game in itself. When the circle is formed, you have the group's attention.

In extreme situations, extreme measures are called for, such as shouting nonsense and acting crazy while making weird body movements until everyone watches you. (In Israel, where everyone talks at once, this was the *only* way to get attention.) Try different things to find out what suits you and what works in a particular situation.

Clear and Concise

Directions that are clear and concise are always appreciated by players. People fall asleep (literally!) or leave if an explanation is too long or complicated. Fuzzy descriptions lead to confusion and at least a million questions and make everyone wish they were somewhere else. This doesn't mean forget telling a (short!) story or making up fantasy tales, but it helps to be organized and usually brief.

Inviting

Always invite onlookers but don't insist that they join. An invitation lets them know they are welcome, even if they don't join. It never hurts to extend another invitation at the start of each game, as long as you don't harass people. Some people respond to coaxing, especially if they secretly want to join, and it presents more than one possibility to easily change their minds.

I have never known of anyone who tried to disrupt or destroy a games session after having been asked to join. In a workshop in Strasbourg, France, a very political woman asked me what I'd do if fascists showed up at our play session. Without hesitation I responded, "I'd invite them to join us." She nearly flipped out. Calmly I explained that the fascists would not join—they're too serious—but if they did, they would be changed in the process since these games are somewhere between democracy and anarchy. This, of course, assumes that they don't come with guns drawn.

Dramatic

Facial expressions, alternating loud and soft speech, and doing mime all help hold the players' interest. Telling a (short!) story or creating a fantasy for a game can increase everyone's anticipation. How you introduce games depends on your style. Experiment. You've nothing to lose. Dare to try something that you ordinarily wouldn't do if it seems like fun to you and see if the other players like it.

Repertoire

When the players are tired, they require a quiet game, When they are restless, an active game is called for. Again, if you are playing yourself, you'll be in close touch with the group's needs. As a person presenting games, you need to know a variety of games to meet the requests of the players for a particular situation. If someone asks, "Do you know a game with animal noises that we can play?" you should be able to respond to it. (Carrying a games list helps.) After a while, as you learn more games, you will be able to think of a game or a way to change one you know to fit any situation.

Demonstrate

The second most important thing to do, after you've made a game safe, is to provide a very graphic demonstration of what happens in the game while you are explaining it. Most misunderstandings are cleared up when players can see what you are talking about acted out. Naturally, for someone who is a little unsure of him/herself it's much easier, not to mention support giving, to demonstrate a game with a partner who already knows the game.

Also, it helps to arrange the players in the formation the game is played in *before* you start to explain the game. If the game is played while in a circle, get everyone in a circle first. Be as concrete as possible. Verbal, and therefore usually abstract, explanations alone are generally unclear. People misinterpret what you say, which gives them a different mental picture of the game. When the game starts, be the first one to do what you're asking others to do, especially if they appear hesitant. This helps build trust as well as providing a clear example to follow.

Conclusion

Now that I've carefully outlined how best to present the games, relax! I've seen people do practically everything "wrong" and the game has still gone well. Asked if they understood the game, the players said, "No, but it was fun!" The main things to remember are caring about your fellow players and enjoying the games yourself. Your concern and enthusiasm are enough to make a games session work if the group is at all open to the idea of play. Try it. You may be surprised at how well it goes.

The experience you gain from this is your guide for what to do in different situations. Making mistakes is perhaps the most effective way

to learn with understanding. It forces you to stop and look at what happened. The British have a saying, "Failure is the pillar of success." You will be less likely to make mistakes if you accept that you will make some. And, a little secret, it's even all right to repeat mistakes— it just means that eventually you'll learn the lesson for sure.

Name Games

*I*f you're like me, you have a terrible time remembering a name, especially if you only hear it once. Presented here are six different ways to learn your fellow players' names and still keep playing. I would not recommend playing these games one after another but probably just a few of them during a two-hour play session. A different one can always be introduced later.

Name Echo (5–40 players)

What's the greatest thing since a quadraphonic 3-D movie starring you? Would you believe a whole group saying and acting out your name exactly as you want? Well, why not?!

First, arrange the group in a circle. Then explain that everyone will take a turn going around the circle in one direction saying his name while making any sound or movement that suits him at the moment. Of course, the presenter (you!) will start thereby providing a demonstration and setting the mood.

You might roar out you name, "R-R-ROLF!" while making ferocious lion-like motions. Or maybe you'd be timid like a kitten, "Rolf." Or a choo-choo train chugging along, "Rolf! Rolf! Rolf! Rolf!Rolf! Woo-Woo!" In any case whenever your five-second-or-less demonstration is over, everyone else simultaneously duplicates or echoes your sound and motion, driving you either to tears, laughter or madness. Or all at once.

Then it's the next person's turn in the circle: "Hei-di," leaping "high" (for "Hei") and descending low in a bow (for "di"), again followed by the echo. This goes on until everyone in the entire circle has had a turn. Ask everyone to try not to repeat any motion already done to make it more interesting. It must be a movement that the group can do. (Forget the splits and flips!)

Name Ripple (5–30 players)

This game also involves a name and a motion, but not your own this time. After we know a few names, we can invent sounds and motions for other people.

Again, we begin with the presenter in the circle, but this time the presenter says someone else's name with a gesture, for instance, "Ker-Ker, sten-sten," while doing cancan kicks. One person at a time repeats the name and kick, going in a chosen direction like a wave until reaching the person whose name is "Kersten." Kersten does not repeat her name and gesture but immediately says someone else's name with a new gesture: "Svveeeeennn," opening her arms wide. The process re-

peats until it gets to Sven, who in turn names someone else with a new sound and motion.

Before starting, it wouldn't hurt to go around and quickly have everyone say their name. The game goes on until everyone has been named at least once. No fair using a name of someone not in the circle!

I Sit in the Grass With My Friend . . . (10–30 players)

Imagine this scene: It's summer, it's warm and the sun is shining. You're outside in the country sitting in the grass with your friends. Suddenly you realize you've forgotten many of your friends' names. Here is a way to help you find out again.

First, arrange everyone in a circle, with all players sitting on something which designates his place, such as a cushion, blanket or shoe. (Chairs can be used when inside.) Leave one place open. The game starts with a race by having both of the people on either side of the open space try to move onto that space, the winner saying as he claims his spot, "I sit," thus leaving free the place where he previously sat. The person who had been sitting next to the winner now moves so that she's next to him again, saying "in the grass," thus leaving her former place free.

This space is in turn filled by the third person in a row (who had been sitting next to the second person to move), who says as she sits "with my friend," and names someone in the circle. The person named gets up and moves to the open place, thereby leaving an open place behind them. This is the signal of the start of another short race between the two people sitting on both sides of the open space. The winner starts again by saying, "I sit."

This is not only a great name game, it's also a lot of fun especially when someone does the wrong thing. Before the actual start, it's a good idea to go around the group once and have everyone give their name.

Let players know that if they don't know a name they can simply point at a person while saying, "with my friend," and the person pointed at says his name as he moves to the open space. Once everyone gets the hang of the game, ask them to speed up. Not only will they learn each others' names, they'll remember them!

Choo-Choo (5–50+ players)

If you've never been given a rousing cheer before in your life, this game is for you! It feels pretty good!

Once again, we start in a circle (surprise!). The presenter starts off by announcing that it's a name game called "Choo-Choo" and starts chugging across the circle by whatever path suits her fancy while making a "choo-choo" train sound.

Eventually she stops in front of someone and says, "Hello. I'm Anneka. What's your name?" The second person replies with his name, "John." Upon hearing this, Anneka the choo-choo breaks into a cheer, alternately raising an arm and leg on each side every time she shouts John's name: "John! John! John, John, John!"

Anneka then runs around, places John's hands on her waist and they chug off together to find a new person to cheer and add to their train. After doing so, they turn around so that John becomes the "engine," with Anneka in the middle and the new person last—the cars in the train change direction each time so that everyone gets to be an engine and caboose once.

If the group is larger than ten people, we may want to split the train into at least two trains or more, depending on the size of the

group, after getting about three or four cars. This is not a game I would normally start a games session with, as it's pretty silly and anyone who is apprehensive might flee. However, once the group has gotten into a playful mood, this game can really loosen them up.

Bumpity-Bump-Bump-Bump (5–50 players)

Most people have trouble saying the name of this game much less playing it, but with a few group practices everyone gets the general idea. Besides, it's fun listening to people try to say it as the game goes on.

Just for variety, let's start off in an oval—most circles we make turn out to be ovals, anyway. The presenter stands in the middle and asks everyone to learn the name of the people on either side of him/her. Then, when the presenter points at someone and says "left" or

"right," the one pointed at must name the person on that side *before* the presenter finishes saying, "Bumpity-bump-bump-bump!"

If he names the person correctly and in time, no problem. However, if he blows it by saying nothing, the wrong name, or even the right name too late, he takes the place of the person in the middle. After a while, have everyone change places, preferably standing next to someone they don't know. This makes the game exciting for those who've learned their neighbors' names and gives them a chance to learn some new ones.

To stretch everyone's mind a little further, we can add the command "middle." When the person pointing says that, the one pointed at must name the pointer.

Also, we can increase the number of people in the middle to further increase the excitement, the number depending on the group size. Since this game is a bit anxiety producing, I wouldn't do it as one of the first few games.

Doctor Memory (5–30 players)

Now to the true test of everyone's power of recall! After having had an adequate chance to learn each other's names (or not, if you're mean), we can ask people to recall everyone else's name from memory. Well, it's not *that* bad, actually.

First, arrange the group in a square or triangle (anything but a circle! I'm tired of circles . . . only if you insist) designating a "good memory" side. Then introduce yourself, "My name is Dale." Simple so far. Ask the person next to you to introduce herself plus you, "My name is Brigette and this is Dale." Each subsequent person must continue to introduce him or herself plus all those already introduced until the cir . . . (oh, that's right, we're not in a circle, are we?), square, triangle, or other figure is completed.

Another version of Doctor Memory involves creating a new name using your name plus a word that starts with the same letter, rhymes or somehow fits with your name. A few examples, "Doctor Dale, Dale Whale,* Hill 'n' Dale." It's amazing how this silly association helps you remember someone's name.

In all fairness, the person who introduces and starts the game should also go last. (You'll be surprised at how you pay attention!)

*When I was a child, kids teased me by calling me "Dale the Whale." Since the ecological movement began, however, whales have become fashionable!

Cooperative Games and Ideas for Making Teams and Choosing Partners

Back when I was in grammar school we always chose sides for team games. Of course, if you were chosen toward the end, or God forbid last, you were seen as among the worst players. It was crushing to self-esteem. You also knew the other players would keep the action away from you as much as possible. For example, in baseball you would play right field, or more accurately, "left out." If the action accidentally did come your way, usually you were so tense about flubbing (or over-relaxed from disuse) that more than likely you would blow it. In the end, you lost the desire to play and quit, whether it happened at the age of six, sixteen or sixty. Fear no more. Here are some playful ways for you to enter cooperative team play.

Cows and Ducks (5–50+ players)

Have everyone gather in close and ask which animals are their favorites. Depending on how many teams or groups you want to form, ask the group to reach an agreement and choose that number of animals. For this explanation, I'll use two animals, cows and ducks. Then have everyone look deep within (for about 2 seconds) to determine whether they are a "cow" or a "duck."

Once they know, they are not to tell anyone. Everyone then closes their eyes and finds their own species by making the sound and movement of the animal they've chosen. As usual with eyes-closed games, make sure someone is watching that no one wanders into a wall or any other obstacle, and don't forget to announce that someone is watching over the herd and gaggle. The game ends when everyone has found their own species, naturally.

Huggie Bear (5–50+ players)

First, we must learn the art of "mingling." To do this, we simply walk about and around each other saying, "Mingle, mingle, mingle . . ." Next, someone who's been designated at the beginning of the game gives a command like "Huggie Bear, color of shirt!" Then everyone with the same color shirt gets together in a group and hugs. (Read on for other suggestions.)

The game usually goes on for four or five mingles until we are ready to form groups or teams for the next game or activity. If you want an exact number in each group, say seven, your last command can be "Huggie Bear, groups of seven."

The Partner Game
(8–50+ players)

You don't have a *partner?* What a pity! If you've ever had the dreaded experience of not being able to find a partner when one was needed, this game is for you.

There are a variety of easy ways to do this. One way is to ask everyone to get together with another person who has a piece of clothing the same color as their own. It could be a sweater, skirt, pants or shirt, socks, shoes, or ...? A similar way is to have everyone find someone who has a physical feature like themselves: same color of eyes, same type of hair, same height or same sex. We could also ask for the opposites of any of these, just to see what happens.

Then again, we can move into personal history and match up by: month or season of birth; first initial of your first or last name; birthplace; city, state, country, continent or planet (!) you are from (the last separates the men—and women—from the whatevers).

We can also get abstract. For instance, everyone is told at the count of three to hold out one, two, or three fingers—then find someone for a partner who has the same number of fingers held out. Or ask everybody to hold up their left or right arm, and find someone who has done the same.

The possibilities are as endless ("How did you get here today? Find someone who got here the same way.") as your imagination—the few presented here are merely to get you started. Naturally, the same techniques can be used to make teams, thus eliminating once and for all the onus of being the last one chosen. You might say these techniques are ways that take the worry out of being close.

Other Suggestions (for forming random groups):

- Favorite sports teams (when you need two teams offer two choices, e.g., Cubs or White Sox)

- Favorite food

- Car preference

- What you ate at a recent meal

- Political preference (WARNING: This can be dangerous!)

- Have all players put their thumbs together pointing upward and then close their eyes. One player, also with eyes closed reaches in the middle and presses down half the thumbs. Players open their eyes and join the "pressed" or "unpressed" team. This can obviously also be used to choose one person to be "it," such as in tag.

How to Adapt Games

In the beginner's Mind there are many possibilities, but in the expert's there are few. The mind of the beginner is needed . . . It is the open mind, the attitude that includes both doubt and possibility, the ability to see things always as fresh and new. It is needed in all aspects of life.

Shunryu Suzuki

Or, "What do I do if a game doesn't work?"

Adapting a game is fun and easy. Any game can be adapted to meet the needs of the group, space or situation. All you have to do is change some part of the game! It is advisable to make only one change at a time to avoid confusion and so that the effect of the transition can be clearly seen. You don't need to feel solely responsible for changing a game. The group generally has plenty of ideas. Your job is to keep the energy of the group focused while getting their ideas out in the open.

What can we change? Following is a list of some key elements of games with several examples and some new situations requiring possible changes for making the game fair and fun for everyone. The first possibility is to make no changes at all. Everybody simply does the best they can and that's good enough. Numerous possible changes are listed on the following pages.

Tables For Changing Games

Sample Game	Game Elements	Examples	New Situation	Possible Changes That Can Be Made
Fire Engine	Players*	ages 20–35	teenagers join the game	• make the game more active • don't use games with too much touching initially • avoid children's stories to introduce the games
Cat and Mice	Players	ages 20–35	active children (ages 5–10)	• simplify rules • extend boundaries • use more fantastic stories to introduce games
Wizards	Players	ages 20–35	elderly	• contract boundaries • make game less physically demanding (e.g., walking)

* For the sake of seeing what we can do to include people in these new situations, I'm assuming that everyone wants to play every game, which is not always the case.

Game				Adaptations
La Ba Doo	Players	able to use limbs	players who do not have full use of limbs*	• require all players to restrict the use of their limbs
Ain't No Flies on Us!	Players	standing	in wheelchairs*	• have standing people play in a crabwalk position • have everyone use wheelchairs
Trust Leap	Players	adults standing	preschool children	• require adults to get on their knees
Robots	Players	sighted	blind*	• have sighted players close their eyes or wear blindfolds for some games
The Partner Game	Players	familiar with each other	strangers	• use games that are guaranteed to randomly mix people • use nonthreatening games to start
Energy Cat and Mice	Players	athletically inclined	nonathletic players	• start with games which require the least skill; create handicaps for skilled players

* One possibility for these "special" populations is to pair each person with one of a "normal" ability level enabling him/her to assist. Also, measures can be introduced to slow down fast games (e.g., walking instead of running).

Sample Game	Game Elements	Examples	New Situation	Possible Changes That Can Be Made
Bear Hunt	Players	average intelligence	mentally handicapped*	• simplify the rules • be prepared to accept a complete change of the game, depending on the players' abilities
Cat and Mice	Action or movement	running	children under five	• have an adult carry or hold hands & run with the child
Three's a Crowd	Action or movement	running	nonathletic people	• change to walking or fast walking • suggest motions which slow people down such as making swimming movements with their arms—"You're in H_2O"
Wizards	Action or movement	running	people on crutches	• have everyone not on crutches hop on one leg, walk backwards, walk, fast walk

* One possibility for these "special" populations is to pair each person with one of a "normal" ability level enabling him/her to assist. Also, measures can be introduced to slow down fast games (e.g., walking instead of running).

Car Wash	Action or movement	crawling	hard surface	• use instead a crouch, crabwalk, or have players stand upright
Cat and Mice	Action or movement	holding, carrying	physically weak people	• allow more than one person to hold at a time
Greeting Game	Action or movement	posture	paraplegics	• have paraplegics use their voices
Sista Paret Ut	Boundaries	no limits	players who run too far	• create limitations, like the edge of the playing field • place rope, shoes, frisbees, jackets & handbags to indicate boundaries
Wizards	Boundaries	no limits	tired players	• make very limiting boundaries
Fire Engine	Boundaries	outdoor area size of tennis court	rain, moving indoors to a smaller space	• change the action, e.g., instead of running, make the movement heel-to-toe, heel-to-toe

Sample Game	Game Elements	Examples	New Situation	Possible Changes That Can Be Made
I Sit in the Grass With My Friend . . .	Environment	outdoor area size of tennis court	rocks, holes, poles, sticks, glass	• remove when possible • move to new location; mark dangerous areas, making them out-of-bounds • or if unable to do the above, warn people to proceed with extreme caution: slow down
Zip, Zap, Pop!	Roles	elimination game	eliminated players who want to play	• have players change roles & stay in the game
Wizards	Roles	tag game	player who can't catch anyone	• introduce a rule whereby the "it" can change roles quickly, like yelling "switch" to reverse roles

Wizards	Roles	participation	spectators who don't want to play	• see if you can include them by asking them if they would: • (1) watch over players in eyes-closed games • (2) see that players stay within boundaries or • (3) watch over small children
Car-Car	Fantasy	all players are coupled	odd number of players	• make one couple a threesome and see what they can create
Ironing Board	Fantasy	all players are coupled	new players arrive	• have them form new twosomes or join existing partners to form threesomes • split partners from old twosomes to pair with new players—original players can explain game
Dead Lions	Fantasy	lying down	all want to go in water	• instead of lying on the ground, players must float—now they are "Dead Sea Lions"

Sample Game	Game Elements	Examples	New Situation	Possible Changes That Can Be Made
Little Ernie	Ritual	repeated movement	energetic children	• have person named in story run around ALL the lines • have children hop or make two-legged jumps
Bear Hunt	Ritual	hearing required	deaf players	• have someone also do the explanation in sign language
A-Rum-Sum-Sum	Ritual	body motions	players with limited mobility	• invent new motions that everyone can do
Detective	Goals	find the leader	someone is unable to guess the leader	• ask leader to change motion more often • give detective more than 3 guesses • let detective stand outside of the circle • add second detective (who doesn't know leader)

Cat and Mice	Goals	catching & holding players	someone who can't be caught	• have the unstoppable player hop, fast walk, or do something to slow him/her down
Friendly Football	Equipment	ball game	no one brought a ball	• improvise—could a Frisbee be used instead? or a bundled-up shirt, or a soft shoe? everything is potential equipment
Three's a Crowd		a tag game	too many players	• make more "its" as needed—if the "its" continually change, have them carry something which identifies them as "it," such as a jacket, ball, etc.

Sample Game	Game Elements	Examples	New Situation	Possible Changes That Can Be Made
Friendly Football	Scoring	highly competitive game	players who don't want to join when score is important	• add two balls • place players in pairs—with an arm around waist or tied together at waist side-by-side, back-to-back, at the legs or arms • give less skilled players a scoring advantage
Doctor Memory	Developmental Skills	game with no motor skills	add: throwing, catching	• the person naming people must throw a ball/object to the person named
Doctor Memory	Developmental Skills	game with no motor skills	add: throwing, skill-catching	• the person naming people must catch and throw with one hand
Doctor Memory	Developmental Skills	game with no motor skills	add: throwing, reaction	• the person naming people must throw to people at random

Doctor Memory	Developmental Skills	game with no motor skills	add: throwing, increased difficulty	• the person naming people must do so while everyone is moving around (for a small group)
Wizards	Developmental Skills	game with few difficult motor skills	add: self-control, jumping, & balance	• have frozen players bend over at waist—unfrozen players must leapfrog over them to free them
Wizards	Developmental Skills	game with few difficult motor skills	building strength and lifting ability	• unfrozen players must pick up frozen mates to free them

Sista Paret Ut (7–21 players)

A game that I often came across in Sweden was "Sista Paret Ut" (Last Couple Out). There were some features of the game which bothered me, thus making it a game to adapt.

In the game, everyone except one stands side by side holding hands with a partner forming two lines facing the same direction. The single caller stands in front also facing forward and yells "Sista paret ut!" The last couple in line then races forward toward the front of the line, one on either side (but a safe distance away). They attempt to reconnect anywhere in front of the line before the caller tags one of them. The caller must wait until he spots one of them before moving.

Everything was fine until there was a caller who was too slow to catch anyone. In fact, it didn't take long for this to happen. This was tiring, embarrassing, and demoralizing. So I asked how we could change the game so that the caller would change regularly. One suggestion was that the caller can be "it" a maximum of five times. Not bad, but there was an implied sense of failure. Another suggestion was more fun. When a couple touched, all three players (including the caller) then raced back to the front of the line. A slow caller was generally closest thereby gaining an advantage, because the last one to arrive was the new caller.

Knots/Giant Knot (10–50 players)

Two games that I almost always use, "Knots" and the "Lap Game," are easily adapted by participants to meet a particular need.

"Knots" is a game where between six and ten players form a tight circle with their hands in the middle. They gently mix up their hands (perhaps with eyes closed) and at a given signal, take two hands. If one takes the hand of the person next to him (too easy!) or both of another person's hands, they break and reconnect with someone else. Once proper connections are made, they are in a knot. The idea is to arrange themselves in a circle without letting go. Naturally, they are not required to break their wrists maintaining a tight grip. Hand contact is all that is necessary.

When there was a large group, I would make as many small circles as needed. This meant that I'd have to stay out of the game dashing back and forth starting the game over or introducing a new one to groups who finished quickly. A way to include everybody in the same game of "Knots" is by starting with everyone holding hands in a circle and gently making themselves into a "Giant Knot." Players keep going over and under arms and around people without letting go of hands until no one can move. Then, unwind back into a circle. Unlike the small knot, we know it's solvable since we began in a circle. Also the presenter can participate (Hooray!).

The Lap Game (2–50 players)

Quite often I close game sessions with the "Lap Game," which visibly connects people, making them interdependent. To play, everybody stands in a circle close to each other facing in. Then everyone turns 90 degrees in the same direction (either left or right) so that they are facing their neighbor's back. Then everyone puts their hands on their neighbor's waist, being careful not to get too close or too far away. The magic words of assistance: "On my knees, please." Then everybody sits, making sure their knees are together, guided by the person in back of them to his knees. Thus you have a seated circle.

Unfortunately, groups of people keep trying to establish the "World Record Lap Game." This appears contrary to the spirit of cooperative games mainly because it's deadly boring waiting while thousands of people get organized. Also, suppose you only have two people? Edith and Erri from Groningen, Holland, invented a variation that guarantees a tie of a record *every* time! "The World's Smallest Lap Game."

Elephant, Rabbit, Palm Tree (10–30 players)

Finally, there is an imaginative variation of the game called "Elephant, Rabbit, Palm Tree." The game goes like this: One person starts in the middle of circle and points at someone and says either "elephant," "rabbit," or "palm tree." The person pointed at becomes the centerpiece and the two adjacent people supply ears or leaves as required. If somebody does the wrong thing, they take the place of the person in the middle.

Challenge can be added by:

- having the middle person count to five (and later to three, as everyone gets quicker), by which time the threesome must be ready
- including a "donkey," where motion is forbidden by the person pointed at as well as the person on either side
- having more than one person in the middle, who point simultaneously.

A more involved and creative variation is to start by dividing the players into groups of as many roles as you want to create, though more than five gets confusing. It could be plants, animals, or situations—anything from ballet to bananas (sorry, Anna!). Then, have these groups present their creations. Have the whole group practice the creations of each group, then play. It's good to start with only a few roles, adding more as people get the hang of those already presented.

My friend Martin from Vienna had a crazy group in Saarbrücken, West Germany, that came up with things like "Fire Engine" with someone acting as a wild driver, someone else climbing a ladder, and the third person twirling an arm in the air for a flashing light while all made a siren wail. With self-entertainment like that, who needs television?

Friendly Football (8–24 players)

Football (soccer, in the U.S.) is probably the most well known and popular sport in the world today. Usually it is played with people of similar ability. Although I've seen fathers play with their sons, I have never seen mothers and daughters included. Again applying the rule that everyone wants to join, we can mess with the rules of the game to find a way that everyone can participate happily. One easy thing you can do is to attach two players by tying one player's right leg to his partner's left leg. You can use shoestrings if nothing else is available, as I once did at the Festival of Fools in Amsterdam.

Perhaps each adult could be attached to a child, or a woman to a man—some way which makes everyone equal. The level of competition declines quickly because no one is expert (unless they normally play that way!) and the pace is considerably slower. It's impossible to take

the game too seriously. If one side is clearly superior, swap a few pairs to even it out.

I *did* say NO equipment was required. No problem. As mentioned under Equipment in charts in the preceding section, many things can be used. I saw players in Scotland using a tin can. No can? Use a paper cup. Your imagination will help you find what you need.

He who laughs, lasts.

attributed to Mary Pettibone Poole

Metalogue: About Games and Being Serious

Daughter: Daddy, are these conversations serious?
Father: Certainly they are.
D: They're not a sort of game that you play with me?
F: God forbid . . . but they are a sort of game that we play together.
D: Then they're not serious!

* * *

F: Suppose you tell me what you would understand by the words "serious" and a "game."
D: Well . . . if you're . . . I don't know.
F: If I am what?
D: I mean . . . the conversations are serious for me, but if you are only playing a game . . .
F: Steady now. Let's look at what is good and what is bad about "playing" and "games." First of all, I don't mind—not much—about winning or losing. When your questions put me in a tight spot, sure, I try a little harder to think straight and to say clearly what I mean. But I don't bluff and I don't set traps. There is no temptation to cheat.
D: That's just it. It's not serious to you. It's a game. People who cheat just don't know how to *play*. They treat a game as though it were serious.
F: But it *is* serious.
D: No, it isn't—not for you it isn't.
F: Because I don't even want to cheat?
D: Yes—partly that.
F: But do you want to cheat and bluff all the time?
D: No—of course not.
F: Well then?
D: Oh—Daddy—you'll *never* understand.
F: I guess I never will.
F: Look, I scored a sort of debating point just now by forcing you to admit that you don't want to cheat—and then I tied on to that admission the conclusion that therefore the conversations are not "serious" for you either. Was that a sort of cheating?

D: Yes—sort of.

F: I agree—I think it was. I'm sorry.

D: You see, Daddy—if I cheated or wanted to cheat, that would mean that I was not serious about the things we talked about. It would mean that I was only playing a game with you.

F: Yes, that makes sense.

* * *

D: But it doesn't make sense, Daddy, It's an awful muddle.

F: Yes—a muddle—but still a sort of sense.

D: How, Daddy? . . .

* * *

F: You brought up two questions. And really there are a lot more . . . We started from the question about these conversations—are they serious? Or are they a sort of game? And you felt hurt that I might be playing a game, while you were serious. It looks as though a conversation is a game if a person takes part in it with one set of emotions or ideas—but not a "game" if his ideas or emotions are different.

D: Yes, it's if your ideas about the conversation are different than mine . . .

F: If we *both* had the game idea, it would be all right?

D: Yes—of course.

F: Then it seems to be up to me to make clear what I mean by the game idea. I know that I am serious—whatever that means—about the things that we talk about. We talk about ideas. And I know that I play with the ideas in order to understand them and fit them together. It's "play" in the same sense that a small child "plays" with blocks . . . And a child with building blocks is mostly very serious about his "play."

D: But is it a *game*, Daddy? Do you play *against* me?

F: No. I think of it as you and I playing together against the building blocks—the ideas. Sometimes competing a bit—but competing as to who can get the next idea into place. And sometimes we attack each other's bit of building, or I will try to defend my built-up ideas from your criticism. But always in the end we are working together to build the ideas up so that they will stand.

Gregory Bateson

Life Is a New Game

Most people do not take playing seriously. On the one hand, that is exactly as it should be—playfulness and seriousness are opposites defining each other. However, this does not mean, as some "serious" people think, that play is superficial and has no real value. Seriously speaking, play is not only fun but deepens and stimulates creative thinking, especially when the player's imagination and ideas are integrated into the games. People get motivated to go past their limits. This creative energy can then be used to solve problems both on a personal and a professional level.

New Games themselves represent only one aspect of the life-as-a-game philosophy, but the idea behind them extends into all areas of living. For example, there are other worthwhile goals besides merely winning, like participating. For the vast majority of people left out of traditional sport and recreation programs, just being able to play New Games is a meaningful victory. Another use of New Games is at work, where a relaxed, playful atmosphere helps build team spirit. This ultimately means more and better work done. Also, mundane tasks such as housework can be given new playful definitions. Finally, I feel that play has a transformative potential for healing and growth.

What happens to people when they play New Games is nothing short of phenomenal. One time while playing in a Stockholm Park, I noticed an elderly Swedish gentleman observing us with interest from across the street. First he came over to our side of the street for a closer look. I invited him to join us. He smiled but shook his head "No." The next time I looked he was even closer and again I asked him to participate. This time he laughed but once more refused. When I next noticed him, he had joined us playing!

Later, he came up to me and said, "When you first asked me to join, I said to myself, 'No, I'm too old.' When you asked the second time, I thought once again, 'I'm too old!' You see, I've been a businessman for forty years and in all that time I never played. But finally I realized, watching you play, 'I'm *not* too old!' and I joined in."

Meet Your Limitations:
Special Populations

The idea of setting limitations for games works in two ways: (1) the leader's expectations and (2) the expectations of the participants. Once, when I was living in San Francisco, I was planning for my first play session with people from a senior citizens' center. I came up with about five games I thought they could do, about six more that I thought *maybe* they could do, and a whole lot more games that I knew there was *no way* they could do. I should mention that I had always been a bit squeamish around old people—reflecting perhaps my own fear of growing old.

When they arrived, much to my dismay, I saw that some were in wheelchairs and others were missing a limb or two. Good lord! I had not counted on that. I had never had a group like this before. I thought,

"What do I do with these people for two whole hours?" First we played the five "safe" games. No problems, but we were finished in twenty minutes. The six "maybe" games were completed in another twenty-five minutes. Now what to do?

The group seemed to be really enjoying themselves, so I thought, "What the heck, why not try some of the games I don't think they can do." After all, I *had* to do *something*. To my surprise, they automatically adjusted the games individually or made suggestions for everyone to follow. For a simple example, when we played "Cat and Mice," which calls for running, they simply went at their own speed, which in some cases meant walking. It didn't seem to dampen their enthusiasm for the game. When one elderly man started wobbling and looked like even walking was too big a challenge, without a word being said someone went over and paired up with the man, giving him support. This showed me that the limitations were more in my own mind than in theirs.

Playing at Work

New Games also has a role in the workplace. The games can be used simply for relaxation or as an energizer during a meeting or conference. Some New Games also have the potential to be used as tools on a deeper level to help solve problems by improving communication, bringing out creativity, and acting as a mirror of the work situation. The latter should be done with sensitivity and only after the group members have developed trust in each other and in what we are doing together. At least a day is required to establish this trust and an ongoing commitment made to maintain it.

For me, the problem-solving and conflict resolution aspects are the most exciting areas of games playing. They are the basis for my latest "new games," which present a real challenge in that they have the potential to go much deeper than any previous work I've done. This can be done with a group after establishing a safe environment with New Games initially used just for fun. The games for the next step of problem-solving and conflict resolution require absolute cooperation to work successfully.

Whatever happens during a game then becomes the subject matter for a reflective discussion examining our own role, that of others, and the group's interactions. Having established an open atmosphere where ideas and opinions flow freely concerning our relations in a game setting, we can then switch over to the work setting to see if the same or different behavior occurs. Needless to say, this is a delicate process which demands sensitivity to make it work.

While in Adelaide, Australia, in 1985, I played with the whole office staff at a Work Preparation Centre for job rehabilitation. At first the men were wearing suits and ties and, along with the women, had looks of doubt on their faces. Their boss was enthusiastic about what playing together could mean to them, but they clearly had not yet caught the play bug.

After one-half hour of playing, though, the suits, ties and odd looks were shed. The "boss" and the lowliest clerk were equals: Their ideas counted just the same. The business manager commented to me later, "We've never had so much fun together. I feel I know the others a bit better now because I got to see a side of them I have never seen before." Though our time together had been brief, it confirmed for me once again that New Games and more advanced play forms belong in the business world.

The Search for Alexander's Nose

However, not every business office can take time to play for a few hours, or even ten minutes, once a week. The New Games Foundation in San Francisco was a prime example. Here we were, an organization dedicated to getting others to engage in cooperative play, and we were so busy that we stopped playing ourselves! "We" had become "them." Like the famous *Pogo* cartoon had said, "We have met the enemy, and he is *us*."

What to do? Everybody claimed that they were overloaded with work, which was true. At about that time a national museum tour, "The Search for Alexander" was in San Francisco. The publicity poster for the show had a bust of Alexander the Great. However, the bust had been damaged, the nose was chipped off. This gave rise to a local joke that the exhibit should be called "The Search for Alexander's Nose." At the same time, someone came into the New Games office wearing one of those Groucho Marx glasses with bushy eyebrows, moustache, *and* a big nose. Removing the nose from the disguise gave us all the elements we needed to invent a game that we could play in the office without significantly upsetting our work. As you may have guessed, we called the game "The Search for Alexander's Nose."

The game is very simple. Someone would hide the "nose" somewhere in the office—everyone else would have to try to find it. We rarely ever searched for it, but eventually someone would come across it. Sometimes it would take ten minutes. Or it could take up to ten days. Hiding places such as among the coffee filters, in the filing cabinets, or in the light fixtures became too easy. Our imaginations were truly stretched.

Whenever it was found the discoverer would proclaim something like, "So, *there's* Alexander's nose!" and everyone would come to see where it had been hidden. The finder then had to hide the nose again for the next round of play. The challenge was to find a place no one else had thought of before. All this took only a minute, but it provided a playful break at the most unexpected times and reminded us why we were working there in the first place.

It didn't take long to exhaust all the obvious locations and also to realize that this was a fun, ongoing game. If a machine jammed there was a good chance it was Alexander's nose. Alexander's nose was discovered one time taped to the underside of the toilet lid. The hiding places became more thoughtful and exotic as time went on. Eventually the boundaries of the office became too small for our game. One staff member went out for muffins and rolls and at that coffee break another staff member bit into Alexander's nose. The coffee shop had baked it into a muffin. Once the nose came in the morning mail with the return address of Alexandria, Virginia.

The game was so much fun we started using it as an example of play in the work setting during our trainings. One time we were doing a workshop in Plano, Texas, just outside of Dallas, and told the trainees about the nose. People responded well and we got into elaborating about all the wild places the nose had turned up. One time someone had emptied out a small cream container and resealed it with the nose inside waiting for the next coffee drinker.

At each workshop we held a public festival where the community was invited to participate in games. The trainees practiced their games leading skills in a true test of fire. During this open play session in Plano a stranger came around asking how to find Nancy Miller, my co-trainer. Upon being introduced he handed her a plain, brown paper bag explaining, "I believe this is yours," and left. Inside was Alexander's nose. A staff member mailed the nose to a relative in Dallas with instructions to deliver it to Nancy.

After the festival when we discussed the experience of leading games Nancy had a great story to tell. When people realized that the very nose they had heard of, had made it to their festival they were ecstatic. A standing ovation greeted the unbagging of the nose.

It's in Your Living Room!
or, A "Clean" Game

This philosophy of play extends beyond New Games or even the New Games office into your home. An example from my own life involves me and my ex-wife, Janka, who then taught computer science at Stockholm University. The problem was that Janka hated to vacuum. At first I didn't mind taking care of it while she did other cleaning. After some months, however, I got a little bored with this routine. I wanted to share more of the housecleaning chores. Janka had unfortunately not developed any great love for vacuuming in the meantime.

At this point I suggested that we make a game out of cleaning house. At first Janka wasn't too enthusiastic if it meant she had to vacuum, but after a couple of tries, we hit on a game we both loved. It went like this: We would start as usual with me vacuuming and her cleaning the bathroom. The difference was that now we had taken the kitchen timer, set it for five minutes, and placed it halfway between where we were working.

When the timer went off, a race would ensue—whoever touched the timer first would get to choose if he/she wanted to change or continue what he/she was doing. The one who lost would get to set the timer for five minutes—or more, so as to catch the winner off guard. What happened was a mad dash every five to ten minutes, with each of us crashing into things on our way to the timer. By the time we both got there, we would usually fall all over each other and collapse in fits of laughter.

After the first few times, it no longer mattered who won. If one of us won two times in a row, we began to joyfully switch jobs anyway, to keep the loser from becoming discouraged. In all honesty, Janka never did become wildly enthusiastic about vacuuming, but the memory of those times at least changed her attitude toward it. She smiled to think about those crazy times, and that already was an improvement.

Player, Heal Thyself!

To state that New Games have a healing potential may sound farfetched to most people. I know from my own experiences, however, that dramatic changes often take place in people who play these games.

One time a man came to a New Games session directly from his job at the American Embassy, where he had had a horrible day. He was upset and angry, and made it plain to me that he was sorry he had promised to join the games. ("Great," I thought, "so glad you could come.")

During the first game he managed a wry smile. By the next game the smile became a grin. By the third game, "Name Echo," where each person in turn presents their name while making a gesture and then has it echoed back to them by the group, he did a silly bow while affecting a British accent. When the group gave him his echo, he roared with laughter. Even after his awful day, the games gave him an opportunity to laugh at himself and restore his sense of balance and humor.

A more dramatic example occurred to me back in 1977 at the time my mother passed on. Two weeks after her memorial service in Chicago I returned to San Francisco. Even before I got into the house I was living in, I learned that the house had been sold and everyone had to move. Then, later that week, a project I had been working on to take New Games into schools fell apart. At the end of the week I received notice that my unemployment benefits had been overpaid, and they proposed cutting them back to twenty dollars per week. At this point, I laughed. After all, what else could happen?

After my second week back I was scheduled to present New Games at a day care center for psychotic patients in my neighborhood. When I arrived I was informed that one of the clients had jumped off the Golden Gate Bridge three days earlier. The clients were understandably upset. It occured to me that we all were in a similar state of mind—I needed a break from my grief, too.

When it came time for me to lead some games, I was introduced to the group. I stood up, but was unable to say or do anything. For the first time, I just didn't feel any energy to begin. After standing for what felt like five minutes, but was probably thirty seconds, one of the male clients ventured to raise his voice and ask, "Hey, are we gonna have any games?" I looked at him and replied with all sincerity, "I hope so." His request was the spark that got me going.

We loosened up with a few games. Since it was warm and sunny and we were right across the street from a beautiful park, I suggested we go outside. Everyone agreed. For the next hour we played and laughed together, gradually forgetting all the heaviness which had been weighing us down. By the end, having gotten some distance from our fears and sorrows, we were ready to face the world again lighthearted and refreshed.

Wheredowegofromhere?

As you may have gathered by now, I do not view play simply. The more I've played New Games and incorporated their philosophy into my own, the more I've found it could be applied to my work, personal, and spiritual life.

Not long after I started presenting New Games, I realized that the games are democratic in that everyone can play regardless of age, sex, or ability. Specifically, this includes mentally and physically handicapped people, grandparents, children, prisoners, business people, anybody! This has led me to be more accepting and tolerant of all kinds of people and their ideas. I no longer feel so judgmental—just as everyone can play New Games, everyone on Earth is part of the game of life.

The most interesting aspect for me currently is introducing New Games in the workplace. The games can be used for superficial reasons such as exercise, energizers, or relaxation. However, after bringing co-workers closer together they can participate in certain cooperative games and exercises which have proven highly successful for facilitating better communication, acting as a stimulus for creative new ideas, and, in a deeper sense, to resolve conflicts.

Also, playful ideas can be practically incorporated into one's everyday life. Daily tasks can be transformed into memorable events and relationships can be improved. As Victor Borge once said, "A laugh is the shortest distance between two people."

Another aspect of games and laughter is their power to heal attitudes and bodies as well. As he has well reported, Norman Cousins attributes the ridding of his collagen disease to greatly increasing his amount of laughter.

Well, wheredoIgofromhere? The New Games philosophy has metamorphosed my view of what is possible: I believe I can achieve anything, given enough time, effort, and spiritual guidance. The first step in making something happen is to *believe* it can happen.

Therefore, my goals are not modest in scope. I plan to take New Games to China and Russia as a means of personal diplomacy. Also, other exotic places I would like to present New Games are Antarctica and outer space, places where good relations are crucial for survival.

Finally, I continue to use play, in the form of visualizations, to find out about the truth of who I am and what I'm on Earth for. Other than being the deepest and most significant dimension of play, I've experienced it as by far the most challenging . . . and fun! That little three letter word is vitally important in my life, for without it, living is like a series of boring classrooms.

It doesn't have to be that way. The key element for me is finding ways (within limits, of course!) to make all the aspects of my life fun.

Where and When You Can Play

Occasionally during my workshops someone will comment, "These games are great, but they would never work with my group." First of all, never say "never." Beyond that, if you say and believe the games won't work, it is almost certain they won't. However, after being told this, I've gone to the groups who would "never" enjoy these games to help co-present them and guess what? I cannot think of a single time that the group didn't like the games. Most often they were quite enthusiastic.

It might help to prepare your group by first announcing that New Games will be presented at a specific date and time. Those who show up will be at least curious and it gives those who are uninterested a chance to avoid the situation. Then again, surprise might be the best tactic. Very few people, unless they're in a real funky mood, are totally against playing. Skeptics often become the biggest enthusiasts.

. . . Scholars have been unable to study [the] "spirit of play," because they fell back on the obvious structural distinction and looked at games instead of at the experience of playfulness. Playfulness, or flow, is not limited by the form of the activity, although it is affected by it . . . People can turn any situation into a flow activity . . . a way of life based on play could be just as normal, or fulfilling, as one based on work and achievement.

Mihaly Csikszentmihalyi

. . . working because you want to is the best sort of play.

Robert Heinlein

Of course, the "real" world is not a series of scheduled play sessions intermingled by other matters. However, it doesn't hurt to think

of ways to integrate play and games into your everyday life. You might suggest doing a game or two before a business meeting to help relax and energize participants. See if you notice a difference in the quality of the meeting.

Or perhaps you can offer a change of pace at a party that's dull, dull, dull! Most students love it when a teacher offers a lesson in the form of a cooperative game. Exercises for physical fitness, occupational therapy, and motor and perceptual skill development are particularly easy to make into game form.

I even remember a San Francisco to New York bus trip that was livened up when the riders asked me to do some games with them in an Ohio restaurant parking lot. Everyone but the restaurant owner was pleased. Now I know we should have invited him to join, which might have at least started a friendly and perhaps playful conversation.

As we got on the bus and it rolled away, our spirits weren't dampened—we continued to play in the bus. This was made a little easier since this was the "Grey Rabbit," an alternative bus, and there were only two seats, the rest of the space was filled with covered foam pads. We played some of the most active games I know, like "Cat and Mice" and "Wizards." There were some adaptations, naturally—we were all on our knees, for instance. I must admit that I was surprised how well it went.

Then, there is always the question which was typified by the woman interviewer from a newspaper in Johannesburg, South Africa: "Besides being fun and including everyone, what's the purpose of these games?" My response, after a short shocked delay, was, "You're really asking that?" Some people have trouble seeing the forest because of all those blasted trees. After all, how many activities of any kind do we have which are truly fun and interesting and open to ALL people in a safe environment? Somehow I have the illusion that this is enough.

People are always looking for some underlying reason behind everything. Actually, to borrow from a cartoon called *The Point,* they don't have to have a point to have a point. You might say that the concept of these games goes UNDER people's heads: it's right there, under their noses! People in the Western world have a tendency to over-intellectualize everything. When a person truly experiences their own spirit of playfulness in any activity it is a moment to treasure—for that moment. Perhaps Csikszentmihalyi (a free taco to anyone who pronounces this name correctly on the first try!), in his book *Beyond Boredom and Anxiety*, says it best:

People who enjoy what they're doing enter a state of "flow": they concentrate their attention on a limited stimulus field, forget personal problems, lose their sense of time and of themselves, feel competent and in control, and have a sense of harmony and union with their surroundings. To the extent that these elements of experience are present, a person enjoys what he or she is doing and ceases to worry about whether the activity will be productive and whether it will be rewarded.

Still, you don't need games or a group to play. Csikszentmihalyi goes on to say:

Conversely, a "flow activity" is an activity that makes flow experiences possible. Such an activity provides opportunities for action which match a person's skill, limits the perceptual field, excludes irrelevant stimuli, contains clear goals and adequate means for reaching them, and gives clear and consistent feedback to the actor . . . The concept of flow makes it possible to see work, and cultural definitions of life style in general, as much more flexible than they are usually thought to be. It allows us to question the necessity of drudgery and anxiety, and it suggests ways in which everyday life can be made more free. There is no reason to believe any longer that only irrelevant "play" can be enjoyed, while the serious business of life must be borne as a burdensome cross. Once we realize that the boundaries between work and play are artificial, we can take matters in hand and begin the difficult task of making our life more livable.

If we continue to ignore what makes us happy, what makes our life enjoyable, we shall actively help perpetrate the dehumanizing forces which are gaining momentum day by day. Enjoyment is left out of the equations for production, rationalization, and behavior control, partly because it has remained for so long a vague concept. Something that cannot be defined can safely be ignored. Instead of enjoyment, leisure is used as an indicator. Leisure, as defined in the various official documents that measure society's collective well-being (see, for instance, Executive Office of the President, 1973), reflects patterns of **consumption** and has nothing to say about personal satisfaction. The number of outboard motors or snowmobiles owned, the quantity of tennis players or theatergoers, does not tell us anything about whether people enjoy their lives.

If the trend toward increased mechanization of life is to be reversed—and social alienation and individual meaninglessness thereby reduced—the first step must be the recognition that there is such a thing as positive enjoyment.

Playing is an attitude which covers every aspect of life including the spiritual. The games presented here are offered as a method of reawakening your playful spirit, which is an aspect of your total spirit. It's up to you to use that rediscovered energy to make your life more flowing and experience it more fully. When you are playing, you're present in the moment here and now, your whole attention is taken up. There's no time for daydreaming or senseless worrying. Viewed this way, everything that happens to you is another element in the game of life.

Dorothy Maclean, one of the founders of the Findhorn Community in northern Scotland, gives us another outlook on playfulness. She relates a message she has received from *devas* (a word from Sanskrit meaning "angels"):

[Devas] present to you most of all a sense of humor, which can operate on all levels at once, which bounces through the universe with the speed of light. Being light itself, it melts and lifts all it contacts. The devas of fun have immense scope, with entry where all else fails. They affect all kingdoms, but in humanity they find fullest range.

It is the greatest privilege to be a deva of this attribute, to see the most dense darkness become light in a flash and open a pathway for myriads of our hosts. From the depths of despair, a smile can appear and a soul feel alive again, ready for change and movement. Time and place become nothing. There are no tortuous roads to climb, for an instant touch of humor transports a soul into another world, a bright hopeful world where anything is possible.

We do not tell you what to do; we are not trying to teach you. We are merely explaining, from our point of view, the wondrous work of fun. God has created all wonders, but perhaps the most magic one of all is when, from the most unexpected place, we see a sudden blaze of light—someone has laughed, and all is well. Negative humans can switch in a second, smile, and see a way again. Those who are stuck in routine, those who draw to themselves all kinds of obstacles, can suddenly see the ridiculous side of life and thereby be freed.

The Newest Games

So far I have been writing about how the spirit of play applies to all aspects of life. For me, that spirit has now come alive in a new and most challenging way—through games that help me look within myself.

Some of these games have been around for thousands of years: tarot, astrology and the I Ching. Some have developed more recently, in forms of modern psychology such as Gestalt, for instance. These games give me a chance to play with ideas about who I am and where I am heading. As such, I have found them to be some of the most exciting and rewarding games I have played.

As in playing any New Game, a person must be open and ready to risk feeling at least a little bit foolish in order to end up feeling a whole lot more alive. The difference in playing these newest games, however, is that they go much further than the games we've been playing so far. Games for developing inner awareness offer players the possibility of seeing themselves more clearly, in a safe context, without defenses.

While these games are the toughest ones I've ever played, I can't remember ever feeling as liberated or having grown as much. I began to become aware of what was happening in my life and relationships, and why. For instance, it was actually through such play that I discovered that my fear of getting too close in a relationship was based on the rejection by my first love twenty years before! My pattern had been that whenever I would start opening my heart to a partner, I would start feeling attracted to other women. This effectively pushed my partner back, guaranteeing my "safety"—and also our unhappiness. Through playing games for self-discovery, I began seeing my unconscious patterns as they started and was able to take steps to consciously change my actions.

In presenting these next games, rather than commenting on them myself, those who created the games will introduce them to you.

We are beginning to learn the creative joy of play. I believe, for example, that all creativity and consciousness is born in the quality of play, as opposed to work, in the quickened intuitional spontaneity that I see as a constant through all my own existences, and in the experience of those I know.

I communicate with your dimension, for example, not by willing myself to your level of reality, but by imagining myself there. All of my deaths would have been adventures had I realized what I know now. On the one hand you take life too seriously, and on the other hand, you do not take playful existence seriously enough.

We enjoy a sense of play that is highly spontaneous, and yet I suppose you would call it responsible play. Certainly it is creative play. We play, for example, with the mobility of our consciousness, seeing how "far" one can send it. We are constantly surprised at the products of our own consciousness, of the dimensions of reality through which we can hopscotch. It might seem that we use our consciousness idly in such play, and yet again, the pathways we make continue to exist and can be used by others. We leave messages to any who come by, mental signposts.

We can be highly motivated therefore, and yet use and understand the creative use of play, both as a method of attaining our goals and purposes and as a surprising and creative endeavor in itself.

Seth/Jane Roberts

EarthLove (4–6 players)

"EarthLove" is a board game, a cooperative process, and an exploration of the Oneness of all life. The game is played as a workshop with a skilled facilitator assisting the participants.

There are many reasons to play "EarthLove"—to have fun, to take time to be with others in an open and attentive manner, to explore deeper aspects of one's self, and to participate in healing the planet by integrating our own experiences.

In terms of the game's rules, the group intention is to move through the Kingdoms of Nature—Mineral, Plant, Animal and Human—to an experience of Oneness with all Life. Players achieve this by rolling a die, moving along the path of experience on the game board, and receiving the game's currency, much like any other game.

What gives "EarthLove" another dimension is that during every turn, players relate an experience from their lives which makes a connection between the "space" they land on and the kingdom they're in. As the game progresses, the synergistic aspects of connectedness become more and more apparent; one player's turn affects others' currency; another player's story moves the group toward Oneness; one person's experience in the Mineral Kingdom stimulates insight for another individual in the Animal Kingdom. Oneness becomes a tangible reality as the game unfolds.

Players' sharings focus on connection—the quality, depth and meaning of our contacts with nature. The definition of relationship is stretched to include crystals, begonias, sparrows and mountaintops besides people. Game players find that inspiration, healing, and humor exist within every form of life, in every Kingdom. As we open ourselves to Earth's wisdom the quality of our own lives is enriched.

The subtle, synchronistic and magical qualities of life are reflected in the game, as well. Participants find that the spaces they land on mirror the patterns of their lives. As the group builds a sense of unity, individual intuition and group synergy emerge.

Experienced "EarthLove" players return to the game for the same reasons they walk in the woods—to connect with themselves, with nature, and with the web of life. Some players bring personal issues to the game, others play solely to liberate the child within. As one nine-year-old workshop participant said, " 'EarthLove' is fun because I get to talk about me, and everybody listens. It is a place to talk about important things like my dog or a bird's nest I found."

Playing the game encourages participants to see themselves as stewards of a sacred earth, a place where every caring thought, every conscious interaction with the natural world helps to build its wholeness. A banker in the city who was a player said, "I am empowered and renewed by 'EarthLove.' It reminds me that although I spend little time in nature, my appreciation of a tree or a bird on my way to work really does matter. I can think of myself as a committed earth steward as I tend to my few houseplants. That's wonderful!"

In the six years since creation of "EarthLove," I have played it in conference rooms, backyards, the Pentagon, two prisons and numerous living rooms and airplanes. I have played it with gardeners, metaphysicians, adults and children in formal and informal settings. While every game is different, reflecting the interests and experience of the participants, every game is also the same, for, given the chance, human beings love to share the deep mystery and wisdom nature expresses.

As more and more of us live busy, urban lives, "EarthLove" offers an opportunity to reflect upon the times when we have been blessed with simple, direct, meaningful communion with the living planet. Recalling and recounting such experiences creates a deepening and centering effect, recreating their magic in the present moment and evoking a tangible experience of the Oneness of all Life.

Making EarthLove

The "EarthLove" game was conceived in 1981, inspired by my years at the Findhorn Foundation in northern Scotland. My deepest area of exploration there was attunement with nature in the garden, and I was inspired by my contact with the birthing of the "Game of Transformation." Upon returning to the U.S. from Scotland I applied the principles of board gaming to our roles as earth stewards and created "EarthLove."

Four years later, I went back to the Findhorn Foundation for a visit, shared the game with members and trained one community member to guide the game. In 1986, Boudewijn Boom, an experienced "game deva" of "EarthLove," and I led a ten-day training at the Findhorn Community for members who wished to deepen their experience of the game and work toward becoming game facilitators. It has been particularly fulfilling to me to "take 'EarthLove' home" to the place where the principles of the game were a part of my living experience and inner life.

Phoebe Reeve

Star + Gate (1–5 players)

"Star + Gate" is both an exciting new system for self-knowledge and an insightful game for stimulating creativity and increasing intuition.

It's used by adults and those of younger ages for solving problems, making decisions and exploring relationships.

The basic card set consists of 96 two-sided symbolic cards, each displaying a simple, evocative visual symbol on one side along with related keywords on the reverse. Following the instructions which accompany the game, the player chooses a topic or question of personal interest, such as "Should I take this job?" or "Improving my relationship with Robert."

The cards are then dealt onto the Sky Spread game board, which contains boxes labeled "You Now," "The Issue," "Helping," and "Distracting," etc. Players develop their own meanings for the cards, using symbols, words and a technique called Picture Stories. The process leads to insights and visualization of the desired results.

The "Star + Gate" system is used throughout the world by people of varied interests and backgrounds as a contemporary and easy-to-learn method similar in some ways to the I Ching or tarot. Many counselors and therapists also use "Star + Gate" as a tool since the game (or method) permits individual interpretation while stressing the value of one's attitude and outlook on life.

Richard H. Geer

The Transformation Game
(2–4 players)

The "Transformation Game" originated at the Findhorn Foundation in Scotland in 1978. As a refined and creative tool which supports and empowers the change processes we all experience, one of the unique gifts of "The Game" is its ability to move swiftly and accurately to the core of any issue. It brings awareness, resolution and healing to current challenges and inspires players to make meaningful and appropriate changes in their lives.

The "Transformation Game" provides a context in which each player sees their life from a wider perspective and observes and assesses particular patterns and attitudes, identifying blind spots or limitations

which might be setting her back on her path, and helping her find new ways of being more effective, joyful and fulfilled. The game mirrors life with accuracy, taking players as deep as they allow it to and teaching lessons as fundamental or extensive as they wish.

The "Transformation Game" responds to any situation presented, shedding light on important personal issues and providing immediate direction for next steps. It is equally beneficial for large or small matters. Whether simple decisions or major life crossroads, the "Transformation Game" provides a doorway through which players can move to discover their own highest truths. In clear, concise and surprising ways it supports players in recognizing their true nature as resourceful and capable agents of personal and planetary change.

When the Foundation began offering the "Transformation Game" workshop it rapidly became one of their most popular programs. Over the years the workshop has been refined and has matured into one of the most sophisticated, integrated and effective tools for raising consciousness. The feedback it provides is superb, and playing "The Game" is acknowledged as a reliable, profound and nurturing way to recognize our deepest truths.

Although it was initially designed to be played in an intimate workshop setting, facilitated by expert guides, one particular aspect of "The Game," the Angel Meditation cards, began to be used outside this framework by players who wanted to incorporate "Game" principles in their everyday lives.

In the fall of '87, after two years of experimentation with a marketable version of the workshop, research culminated in the production of a simplified, do-it-yourself "Game." The new, streamlined "Transformation Game" retains the best of the parent "Game" workshop. Its original essence has been enhanced by the levity and brevity characteristic of a home game in a comfortable, personal setting.

While "The Game" can be played just for fun, it also responds to a more serious approach. As a powerful interactive tool, it fosters cooperation and group sharing. Also, it helps players to solve problems, move past limits, achieve desired goals and deepen understanding. Each "Transformation Game" includes a Next Step pad enabling players to gain immediate direction for any issue they are currently facing without playing an entire game.

The wisdom, clarity and insight of "The Game" have a beneficial application in all aspects of life—personal, social, emotional, financial, medical, environmental, psychological, educational and spiritual. Its appeal to a varied cross-section of people around the world reflects the need for broadly based self-realization tools which can bridge the inner and outer worlds and bring new meaning, pleasure and enrichment to the quality of our lives. Whatever lies ahead for all of us, it is apparent that moving forward with acceptance, a light heart, and the support and understanding of friends, will help us to shape our future with joy, harmony and grace.

Joy Drake

Developmental Skills

If it has not been obvious until now, I'll state it plainly: the point of these cooperative games is NOT FOR TRAINING of specific skills. They are mainly JUST FOR FUN! However, at even a casual glance, it is obvious that many skills and features are naturally involved.

Let's say, for instance, that a teacher or physical education instructor has just given a test, exercise, or workout. Neither the teacher nor the students want anything too challenging to do, but the instructor would like to present something which uses certain skills and imagination while being a lot of fun. These games, sometimes with slight adaption, are perfect!

The chart that follows is made solely of key elements according to the games' descriptions as given in this book. They are shaded. Those games which contain these as secondary elements are indicated with X's. To repeat again, any game can be changed to include or accentuate certain specific elements. Please refer to the section "How to Adapt Games" for examples of this (particularly the last examples, which relate to skills).

There are four areas of Developmental Skills represented in the games that we will consider here: Social Behavior, Individual Behavior, Physical Features and Basic Motor Skills. This system is based on ideas in Gerhard Hecker's book, *Kompendium Didaktik Sport.*

DEVELOPMENTAL SKILLS	cooperation—working together for a common goal	trust—building a feeling of group safety	problem solving—finding one out of many possible solutions
A-Rum-Sum-Sum	X		
Ain't No Flies on Us!			
Bear Hunt	X		
Blind Run	▨	▨	
Bumpity-Bump			
Captain Video			
Car-Car	X	▨	
Car Wash	X	X	
Cat & Mice	▨		
Choo-Choo	X		
Cows & Ducks	X X	X	X
Dead Lions			▨
Detective	▨		X
Doctor Memory		X	
EarthLove	▨		X X
Elephant, Rabbit, Palm Tree			X X
Energy	▨		
Face Pass			X
Fire/Trust Leap	▨	▨	
Fire Engine	X		
Friendly Football	X X		X
Fruit Basket	X X		

164

verbal contact—interaction with speech (includes listening skills)	X	X			X		X			X	X		X			X	X
tactile contact—physical touching		X		X	X		X	X		X	X		X	X			
adaptability—responsiveness to fit the actions and movements of others	X	X		X	X	X	X	X	X	X	X	X	X		X		X
INDIVIDUAL BEHAVIOR																	
self-control—ability to direct one's body, speech, and mind	X	X		X	X		X			X	X	X	X		X		X
creativity—using one's ideas inventively				X	X		X	X	X	X	X	X		X		X	
spontaneity—impromptu action without special directions given				X		X		X	X		X				X		
pantomime—expression through acting movements				X	X		X	X					X				X

Game	visual ability—observation and peripheral perception	Skillfulness & coordination—complex body movements	reaction—quick physical response	speed—quickness in running
PHYSICAL FEATURES				
Fruit Basket	▒	X	▒	X
Friendly Football	X	X	X	▒
Fire Engine		X	X	▒
Fire/Trust Leap	X			
Face Pass	▒			
Energy			X	
Elephant, Rabbit, Palm Tree	X	X	▒	
EarthLove				
Doctor Memory				
Detective	▒	X		
Dead Lions				
Cows & Ducks				
Choo-Choo		X		
Cat & Mice	X	X	▒	▒
Car Wash		X		
Car-Car	▒	X	X	X
Captain Video	▒			
Bumpity-Bump			▒	
Blind Run		▒		▒
Bear Hunt	X	▒		
Ain't No Flies on Us!				
A-Rum-Sum-Sum	X	▒		

166

strength															░		X	
endurance										X					X		X	X

BASIC MOTOR SKILLS

running		X				░									░		X	X
jumping				░						X						X░	X░		
balance		X																	
climbing																			
leaning on		░																	
crawling		░																	

DEVELOPMENTAL SKILLS	cooperation—working together for a common goal	trust—building a feeling of group safety	problem solving—finding one out of many possible solutions
The Greeting Game	X		(shaded)
Huggie Bear	X		
I Sit in the Grass . . .	X		X
Ironing Board		X	
Knots/Giant Knot	(shaded)		(shaded)
La Ba Doo	X		
The Lap Game	(shaded)	(shaded)	
Little Ernie			
Name Echo	X		
Name Ripple	X		
The Partner Game			
Pyramids		X	
Quack!			
Robots			
Sista Paret Ut			
Star + Gate			
Transformation	(shaded)		
Three's a Crowd			
Wizards	X		
Zip, Zap, Pop!	X	(shaded)	X
Zoom	X		X

168

verbal contact—interaction with speech (includes listening skills)	X	X		X	X		X		X		X	X			X	
tactile contact—physical touching			X	X				X				X	X			X
adaptability—responsiveness to fit the actions and movements of others			X	X	X		X							X	X	

INDIVIDUAL BEHAVIOR

self-control—ability to direct one's body, speech, and mind	X		X	X			X	X			X		X	X		X
creativity—using one's ideas inventively				X	X		X				X	X			X	
spontaneity—impromptu action without special directions given				X			X							X		
pantomime—expression through acting movements	X		X	X												X

PHYSICAL FEATURES	visual ability—observation and peripheral perception	Skillfulness & coordination—complex body movements	reaction—quick physical response	speed—quickness in running
The Greeting Game	X	X	X	
Huggie Bear	X		▨	
I Sit in the Grass . . .	X	X	▨	
Ironing Board				
Knots/Giant Knot	X	▨		
La Ba Doo		X		
The Lap Game		X		
Little Ernie			X	X
Name Echo	X	X		
Name Ripple	X	X	X	
The Partner Game				
Pyramids				
Quack!	X	X		
Robots				
Sista Paret Ut	X		▨	▨
Star+Gate				
Transformation				
Three's a Crowd				
Wizards	▨	▨	▨	▨
Zip, Zap, Pop!	X		X	
Zoom			X	

strength					X				
endurance	X	X		X X X		X		X	
BASIC MOTOR SKILLS									
running		X		X		X			
jumping		X	X						
balance			X X						
climbing	X		X						
leaning on	X						X	X X	
crawling									

Resources

Dale N. LeFevre and his colleagues can be reached at the address below to **lead New Games at Festivals,** to present **New Games Leadership Seminars** and to work as **management consultants with businesses and organizations** in the areas of **Team Building and Conflict Resolution**. Also available is *The New Games Video.* The last three are briefly outlined below, though more information is available upon request.

New Games Leadership Seminars

For those who are interested in learning and leading New Games, you may either schedule a workshop for your organization or find out the current schedule of workshops that you may individually attend. Key areas touched upon are finding a balance between competition and cooperation, establishing the mood for play and finding ways for including everyone who wants to join.

Team Building, Conflict Resolution for Organizations

New Games and related activities offer new opportunities to build trust by creating positive feelings between colleagues. This is the key for resolving conflicts and making a unified team. Play provides a starting point for looking at the real problems. Various processes are then used to explore the blocks which are inhibiting cohesive functioning, and getting beyond the issues that appear to be causing division between people, thereby improving relationships.

The New Games Video

Thirty of the most popular New Games are presented in an easy-to-follow form. The games are explained, demonstrated and, to give you an idea what they look like, briefly played. A succinct written description of each game is included. The hour-long video is divided into three twenty-minute sections: 1. Ice Breakers: Games to Get Acquainted; 2. Sensitivity and Trust Games: Team Building; 3. Games with a Variety of Activity Levels.

New Games

Attn: Dale N. LeFevre
P.O. Box 1641
Mendocino, CA 95460

For further information about the **Transformation Game,** weekend **Game Workshops** and **Angel Meditation Cards**, please contact:

Joy Drake/Kathy Tyler
Innerlinks
P.O. Box 16225
Seattle, WA 98116-0225

For more information about the **EarthLove** game workshops, **Celestial Blessings** or the **Allies** card deck, please contact:

EarthLove
Phoebe Reeve
6810 Murray Lane
Annandale, VA 22003

For information about STAR + GATE contact the publisher. Also available is the book STAR + GATE *Keys to the Kingdom,* a complete guide to the STAR + GATE system. Other titles include the *Circle Pattern,* which displays relationships among the Symbolic Cards, *Diary of Discovery,* a journal for recording STAR+GATE layouts, and a deluxe bookshelf edition.

STAR+GATE Enterprises
P.O. Box 1006
Orinda, CA 94563
Phone: (415) 284-3355

Recommended Reading

James Carse, *Finite and Infinite Games*, Free Press.
Fluegelman & Tembeck, *The New Games Book* and *More New Games*,
  Doubleday.
George Leonard, *The Ultimate Athlete*, Avon.
Terry Orlick, *The Cooperative Sports and Games Book*, Pantheon.
Weinstein and Goodman, *Playfair*, Impact Publications.

About the Author

It is not necessary to be crazy to be a writer, but it's useful. *Anon.*

Suffer fools gladly; they may be right. *Holbrook Jackson*

Dale N. LeFevre was born an August 4, 1946, at his grandparents' farm near Lena, Wisconsin. He grew up on a farm in Wisconsin and in the suburbs of Chicago, Illinois, later graduating from Valparaiso University (Indiana) with a B.S. in Marketing and Management. Though his succeeding education was living in New York City, Dale also received an M.A. in Education from New York University.

In 1975 Dale moved to San Francisco to become the organizer of the Third New Games Festival held in Golden Gate Park, the first time this was done in an urban setting. In his two years with the New Games Foundation, he served as office manager, associate director, and workshop leader.

In the autumn of 1976, Dale formed his own project, Play Express, to take New Games into schools. He traveled in 1977 to give a course at the Open University in Britain, thus beginning a life of international work and travel. Since then, he has given workshops or presentations in over twenty-five countries, including almost every country in Europe. Of special note were playing with Catholics and Protestants in Northern Ireland, mixed races in South Africa, Muslims and Hindus in India, Jews and Arabs in Israel, and church congregations in East Germany. Most recently, Dale has worked in Japan, Australia and New Zealand. Dale's book of poetry called *California (without grapefruit),* is available through him.

This, Dale's first book of New Games, was originally called *Playing for the Fun of It* and available in five languages. He also made a film of New Games for Swedish television. Recently Dale co-produced *The New Games Video* to complement the New Games books. He also made *Cooperation in Corporations* for use in the business setting. The first demonstrates and teaches New Games while the latter focuses on leadership and using games in business. Both encourage participation.

*Return to the beginning;
become a child again.*

Tao Te Ching